GREAT COOKING MADE EASY

MEALS IN MINUTES

Better Homes and Gardens
TRADEMARK

TREASURE PRESS

BETTER HOMES AND GARDENS BOOKS

Editor Gerald M. Knox
Art Director Ernest Shelton
Managing Editor David A. Kirchner
Project Editors James D. Blume, Marsha Jahns
Project Managers Liz Anderson, Jennifer Speer Ramundt, Angela K. Renkoski

Shortcut Main Dishes (American edition)
Editor Joyce Trollope
Project Manager Mary Helen Schiltz
Graphic Designer Lynda Haupert
Electronic Text Processor Donna Russell
Photographers Michael Jensen, Sean Fitzgerald
Food Stylists Suzanne Finley, Dianna Nolin, Janet Herwig, Maria Rolandelli
Contributing Editor Sandra Mosley

Meals in Minutes (British edition)
Project Managers Liz Anderson, Jennifer Speer Ramundt
Assistant Art Director Tom Wegner
Contributing Project Editors Irena Chalmers Books, Inc., and associates: Jean Atcheson, Irena Chalmers, Ann Chase, Mary Dauman, Cathy Garvey, Mary Goodbody, Terri Griffing, Margaret Homberg, Kathryn Knapp, Stephanie Lyness, Susan Anderson Nabel, Victoria Proctor, Elizabeth Wheeler
Electronic Text Processors Alice Bauman, Kathy Benz, Paula Forest, Vicki Howell, Mary Mathews, Joyce Wasson

This edition first published in Great Britain in 1989 by:

Treasure Press
Michelin House
81 Fulham Road
London, SW3 6RB

© Copyright 1986, 1989 by Meredith Corporation, Des Moines, Iowa, U.S.A. All rights reserved. No part of this publication may be reproduced, stored in a retrieval system, or transmitted in any form or by any means, electronic, mechanical, photocopying, recording, or otherwise, without the prior permission of the Copyright owner.

Original edition published by Meredith Corporation in the United States of America.

BETTER HOMES AND GARDENS is a registered trademark in Canada, New Zealand, South Africa, and other countries.

ISBN 1 85051 431 3

Produced by Mandarin Offset
Printed and bound in Hong Kong

We know that you're busier than ever these days, with little time to cook. However, you *can* prepare—and enjoy—delicious meals by using some simple shortcuts. The help you need to start saving time in the kitchen is right here in this book. It was conceived in American kitchens where saving time and making good use of convenience foods have become national passions.

Each recipe in *Meals in Minutes* comes with a timetable to help you plan your own cooking schedule. A quick glance at the recipe reveals just how much time to allow.

In this book you'll also find a variety of practical, timesaving cooking techniques to get you out of the kitchen *fast*. Make use of ready-to-serve foods and learn how to assemble a one-dish frying pan meal. Give yourself a head start by storing an *extra* meal in your freezer. Or, use your slow cooker, oven, microwave, grill, or wok to simplify your cooking. These shortcuts will mean you have more time for the things you really enjoy!

Contents

Introduction
3

Fix-It-Fast Sandwiches
6

Layer favourite ingredients together for casual meals.

Assemble a Salad
12

Start your main dish with ready-to-use salad ingredients. Add creative touches and hey presto—a refreshing supper.

No-Fuss Oven-Frying
46

Coat a variety of meats in this easy, trouble-free way, then cook them in the oven.

Slow Cooker Meals
52

Try your hand at no-hassle cooking. Shift dinnertime preparations to earlier in the day with this slow-cooking appliance.

Fast Frittatas
58

Fix these one-step, open omelettes for supper. They come in a variety of flavours—and they're even simple to serve.

Quick-Cooked Frozen Fish
64

Poach frozen fish for an easy-to-make main dish. The shortcut? You don't need to thaw the fish before cooking.

Sensational Stir-Frys
96

Master the stir-frying technique and you're on your way to super quick and easy cooking.

Skip-a-Step Pasta
104

No need to cook pasta and sauce separately. Bake them together in a single dish.

Fix-and-Forget Oven Meals
110

Want some time off while the meal cooks? An oven meal is your answer. A timetable guides you through the preparation.

Shortcut Buying
118

Special Helps
Become a time-efficient food shopper with these hints.

Off-the-Shelf Recipes
18

Keep ingredients on hand in your cupboard, freezer, and refrigerator. Then create a meal in short order.

Hurry-Up Meat Loaves
26

The shape makes the difference when you're trying to streamline the cooking time of meat loaves.

Speedy Frying Pan Suppers
32

Preparation and serving are both simple for these one-dish frying pan meals.

Streamlined Soups
40

Ladle out a bowl of homemade soup. The soups all take 40 minutes or less to make.

Versatile Meat Make-Aheads
70

Start off with a basic minced meat mixture, then turn it into a variety of delicious supper dishes.

Double-Duty Entrées
78

Save time by cooking in double batches—one to serve now and the other for another meal.

Kabobs on the Grill
84

Add a new shape to your menu and serve quick-cooking kababs. They're like a meal-on-a-skewer.

Convenient Quiches
90

It's the unique "crusts" and simple fillings that make these quiches so special.

The Know-How Of Freezing
120

Special Helps
Save time and money by storing your meat purchases properly.

Nutrition Analysis Chart
122

Index
125

Fix-It-Fast Sandwiches

For impromptu picnics, garden lunches, or light suppers, our sandwiches are unbeatable—and so-o-o-o easy! No cooking. No mess. No fuss. Simply stop at the delicatessen for the ingredients. Then assemble your sandwich choice and you've got a great-tasting meal. For speedy clearing up, use paper plates.

Family-Size Hero Sandwich

Family-Size Hero Sandwich

A giant sandwich for giant appetites!

1 16-ounce (450g) loaf of French bread (16 to 20 inches [38 to 45.5cm] long)
  Mayonnaise *or* salad cream
  Prepared mustard (optional)
  Butter *or* margarine, softened
2 tomatoes
  Lettuce leaves
16 ounces (450g) purchased coleslaw, drained
8 ounces (225g) sliced boiled ham *or* sliced luncheon meat
16 ounces (450g) purchased marinated cucumbers and onions, drained
4 ounces (110g) sliced salami *or* sliced pepperoni

1 Using a fork, lightly scrape and remove the bread from bottom half of the loaf, as shown. This makes more room for the sandwich filling. Leave a ½-inch-thick (1cm) shell of crust and bread to give the sandwich support. If desired, also remove some of the bread from the top half of the loaf. Freeze the crumbs for toppings or meat loaf.

Cut bread in half horizontally with a serrated or sharp, thin-bladed knife. Using a fork, hollow out centre of bottom half of bread; leave a ½-inch-thick (1cm) shell (see photo 1). Hollow out top of bread, if desired. Spread cut side of top half of bread with mayonnaise or salad cream and mustard, if desired. Spread cut side of bottom half with butter or margarine.

Cut tomatoes into thin slices (see photo 2). Arrange lettuce over bottom half of loaf. Layer drained coleslaw, ham or luncheon meat, tomato, drained cucumbers and onions, and salami or pepperoni over lettuce (see photo 3). Place top half of bread on sandwich. Secure sandwich with 6-inch (15cm) skewers and slice sandwich into six portions (see photo 4). Serve immediately. Makes 6 servings.

Assembling time: 20 minutes

2 To remove the stem end from tomato, cut out a cone-shape piece with a sharp knife. To slice the tomato, grasp it with one hand and place it on a cutting board. Use the sharp knife to thinly slice tomato crosswise, as shown.

3 After spreading the bottom half of the loaf with butter, top it with lettuce. Next, layer coleslaw, ham, tomato, drained cucumbers and onions, and salami.

4 Insert 6-inch (15cm) skewers vertically through the top layer of bread, the filling, and the bottom layer of bread. This helps hold the sandwich together while you slice it. If you can't locate 6-inch (15cm) skewers, break longer bamboo kabab skewers into 6-inch (15cm) lengths. Steadying the sandwich with one hand, cut it into portions with a serrated or sharp, thin-bladed knife using a smooth sawing motion, as shown. Remove the skewers before eating.

Cheese and Pastrami Hoagies

- 3 fluid ounces (75ml) natural yogurt
- 2 teaspoons horseradish mustard *or* hot horseradish sauce
- 4 bread rolls (5 to 6 inches [13 to 15cm] long)
  Butter *or* margarine, softened
- 1 small onion
  Lettuce leaves
- 5 ounces (150g) very thinly sliced pastrami *or* cooked beef
- 3 ounces (75g) Gouda cheese
  Whole sweet cherry peppers *or* whole hot banana peppers (optional)

In a small bowl stir together yogurt and horseradish mustard, then set aside. Cut rolls in half horizontally. Using a fork, hollow out centres of bottom halves; leave a ½-inch-thick (1cm) shell (see photo 1, page 8). Spread cut side of bottom halves of rolls with butter or margarine.

Cut onion crosswise into thin slices, then separate into rings. Arrange lettuce leaves over bottom halves of rolls. Layer pastrami or beef, cheese, and onion rings over lettuce (see photo 3, page 9). Spoon yogurt mixture over onion. Replace top halves of rolls. Secure sandwiches with 6-inch (15cm) skewers (see photo 4, page 9). Serve with cherry or banana peppers, if desired. Makes 4 servings.

Assembling time: 15 minutes

Deli Salad Sandwiches

- 12 slices raisin bread
- ¾ pound (350g) purchased chicken *or* ham salad
- 8 ounces (225g) tinned crushed pineapple, drained
- 2 ounces (50g) broken pecans or walnuts

Toast bread. In a small bowl combine chicken or ham salad, pineapple, and pecans. Spread *each* of six toast slices with about *4 ounces (110g)* of mixture. Top each with another toast slice. Secure with toothpicks, then cut sandwiches in half (see photo 4, page 9). Serve sandwiches immediately. Makes 6 servings.

Assembling time: 15 minutes

Stuffed Pitta Pockets

- 8 ounces (225g) purchased potato salad
- 2 teaspoons horseradish sauce
- 3 large pitta bread rounds
- 1 tomato
- 6 ounces (175g) sliced cooked beef *or* ham
- 6 ounces (175g) muenster *or* white cheese, cut into 6 slices
  Lettuce *or* spinach leaves

In a bowl stir together potato salad and horseradish. Mash mixture slightly with a fork, if desired. Cut pitta bread rounds in half crosswise, then separate carefully to form pockets. Cut tomato into thin slices (see photo 2, page 9). To assemble each sandwich half, spoon potato salad mixture into pitta pockets, then add beef or ham, cheese, lettuce or spinach, and tomato. Makes 6 servings.

Assembling time: 30 minutes

Easy Reubens

Want to use pitta bread instead of rye? No problem. Cut two large pitta bread rounds in half crosswise, then line them with cheese and lettuce. Add the filling and pickled cucumbers.

8 ounces (225g) sauerkraut
8 ounces (225g) thinly sliced cooked corned beef
3 fluid ounces (75ml) Thousand Island salad dressing
2 slices Swiss cheese
8 slices rye bread
   Red-tipped lettuce leaves (optional)
4 to 8 gherkin slices

Rinse sauerkraut, then drain thoroughly. Snip sauerkraut with scissors, if desired. Slice corned beef into bite-size pieces. In a medium bowl stir together sauerkraut, corned beef, and salad dressing. Cut cheese slices in half.

To assemble sandwiches, place cheese atop *four* of the bread slices. If desired, add a lettuce leaf. Layer corned beef-sauerkraut mixture on top of lettuce, then layer gherkin slices on each sandwich (see photo 3, page 9). Top with remaining bread slices. Secure with toothpicks, then cut sandwiches in half (see photo 4, page 9). Makes 4 servings.

Assembling time: 15 minutes

Turkey Club Sandwiches

12 slices pumpernickel *or* rye bread
    Prepared mustard
4   ounces (110g) thinly sliced Swiss *or* Gouda cheese
8   ounces (225g) thinly sliced cooked turkey breast
4   fluid ounces (110ml) cranberry sauce
    Lettuce leaves
    Butter *or* margarine (optional)

Toast bread. For top layer, spread *four* of the toast slices with mustard. Layer cheese atop mustard-spread bread. Using *half* of the turkey, layer slices over cheese (see photo 3, page 9).

For bottom layer, spread *four* more toast slices with cranberry sauce. Top with lettuce leaves and remaining turkey.

To assemble sandwich, stack cheese-and-turkey layer on top of each sauce-turkey layer. Spread remaining toast with butter or margarine, if desired. Place buttered side down on each cheese-and-turkey layer. Secure each sandwich with toothpicks, then cut diagonally into quarters (see photo 4, page 9). Makes 4 servings.

Assembling time: 20 minutes

Assemble A Salad

A main-dish salad is a great choice when you need a refreshing meal at short notice. And when you plan to include some ready-to-use ingredients—such as prepared coleslaw or potato salad, bottled dressing, and tinned meat, fruit, or vegetables—it's especially easy to do.

Accompany your meal with rolls or water biscuits, fresh fruit, and a warm drink.

Seafood Louis

Assemble a Salad

Seafood Louis

- 2 tablespoons frozen whipped dessert topping
- 8 ounces (225g) tinned artichoke hearts
- 2 hard-boiled eggs
- 1 large head little gem lettuce
- ½ medium head iceberg lettuce
- 2 large tomatoes
- 8 fluid ounces (225ml) Thousand Island salad dressing
- 1 small lemon
- 6 ounces (175g) frozen crab-flavoured fish sticks *or* frozen cooked prawns, thawed

Place topping in a small bowl and thaw. Place tin of artichokes in the freezer to chill for 20 minutes (see tip, page 16). To hard-boil eggs, place eggs in a saucepan. Cover with cold water. Bring water to the boil. Reduce heat to just below simmering, then cook, covered, for 15 minutes. Drain and cool eggs (see photo 1).

Meanwhile, rinse little gem and iceberg lettuce; drain. Shred iceberg lettuce (see photo 2). Cut tomatoes into wedges. Peel and slice eggs. For dressing, stir salad dressing into thawed whipped dessert topping (see photo 3). Cut lemon into wedges.

Cut crab-flavoured fish sticks into large pieces. Drain artichokes, then cut into quarters. Assemble salads (see photos 4–7). Spoon dressing over salads. Garnish with eggs. Sprinkle with paprika, if desired. Pass lemon. Serves 4.

Assembling time: 35 minutes

1 To quickly cool hard-boiled eggs, place in a pan of cold water and add ice cubes. Then let eggs stand about 5 minutes. Do this as one of the first steps in preparing the salad, so the eggs will be completely cooled when you're ready to use them.

2 After removing the core and rinsing the lettuce, drain in a colander or on kitchen paper.
To shred iceberg lettuce or cabbage, place the half-head of lettuce on a cutting board. Cut into thin shreds with a long-bladed knife.

3 For a creative, quick dressing, in a small bowl stir together Thousand Island salad dressing and thawed whipped dessert topping.

4 Line four small, chilled plates with little gem lettuce leaves.

5 Next, make a pile of shredded iceberg lettuce in the centre of each plate.

6 Place the crab-flavoured fish pieces or cooked prawns on top of the shredded lettuce.

7 Finally, arrange tomato wedges and artichoke heart quarters on salads.

Chicken and Fruit Salad

Substitute tuna for the chicken chunks and voilà... a fruity seafood salad.

  8 ounces (225g) tinned peach slices
10 ounces (275g) cooked chicken, cut into chunks
14½ ounces (410g) tinned grapefruit sections
  1 avocado *or* 1 large apple
     Lemon juice
  4 ounces (110g) soft cream cheese
  ½ teaspoon poppy seed
3½ ounces (85g) shredded lettuce

Place peaches, chicken, and grapefruit in the freezer to chill for 20 minutes (see tip below). Meanwhile, halve avocado lengthwise, then twist gently to separate. Remove seed and the peel, then cut avocado into 12 lengthwise slices. Brush avocado with a little lemon juice to prevent darkening. (*Or,* core the apple and cut it into 12 slices.)

Drain peaches, reserving *3 tablespoons* of syrup. For dressing, stir together reserved syrup, cheese, and poppy seed (see photo 3, page 15).

Place lettuce on four chilled individual luncheon plates (see photo 4, page 15). Arrange chicken in centre of each plate atop lettuce (see photo 5, page 15). Arrange peach and grapefruit sections around edges of the plates (see photo 7, page 15). Arrange avocado or apple slices between chicken and fruit. Drizzle dressing over salads. Serve at once. Makes 4 servings.

Assembling time: 35 minutes

Crunchy Tuna Salad

Oranges, tuna, coleslaw, and nuts is an unusual combination but tastes great.

11 ounces (310g) tinned mandarin oranges
  8 ounces (225g) tinned tuna
16 ounces (450g) purchased coleslaw
     Lettuce
  2 ounces (50g) sliced almonds, peanuts, *or* cashews

Place tins of oranges and tuna in the freezer to chill for 20 minutes (see tip below). Meanwhile, if coleslaw is very wet, drain off excess liquid. Rinse lettuce; drain (see photo 2, page 14). Line four chilled individual salad bowls with lettuce leaves (see photo 4, page 15).

Drain oranges and tuna (see tip, page 21). Break tuna into chunks.

In a bowl gently toss together oranges, coleslaw, and almonds, peanuts, or cashews. Spoon mixture into centre of each lettuce-lined bowl (see photo 5, page 15). Make an indentation in centre of mixture. Arrange tuna chunks in the indentation. Makes 4 servings.

Assembling time: 30 minutes

A Chilling Fact

Many salads call for chilled tinned ingredients. If you're short on time, quick-chill ingredients in the tin in the freezer for about 20 minutes. Or, if you can plan ahead, put ingredients in the refrigerator overnight to chill.

Ham and Macaroni Coleslaw

See photo 2 on page 14 for suggestions on shredding cabbage.

- **8 ounces (225g) corkscrew macaroni**
- **6 fluid ounces (165ml) mayonnaise *or* salad cream**
- **4 fluid ounces (110ml) lemon yogurt**
- **6 ounces (175g) sliced ham**
- **12 ounces (350g) shredded cabbage**
- **4 ounces (110g) grated cheddar cheese**
- **6 ounces (175g) seedless red *or* green grapes, halved**

Cook macaroni according to packet directions; drain. To chill macaroni quickly, place it in a colander, then set colander in a large bowl of ice water about 3 minutes or until cool.

Meanwhile, for dressing, in a small bowl stir together mayonnaise or salad cream and lemon yogurt (see photo 3, page 15). Set aside. Cut ham into bite-size strips.

Place ham, cabbage, and cheese in a large salad bowl. Drain macaroni well, then add to cabbage mixture. Pour dressing over cabbage mixture, then toss to coat well. Arrange grapes atop salad. Makes 4 servings.

Assembling time: 25 minutes

Salmon Potato Salad

- **16 ounces (450g) tinned salmon**
- **1 cucumber**
- **Lettuce**
- **1½ pounds (700g) purchased potato salad**
- **2 ounces (50g) sliced stoned ripe olives**

Place tin of salmon in the freezer to chill for 20 minutes (see tip, page 16). Meanwhile, score cucumber, if desired. To score cucumber, run prongs of a fork lengthwise along unpeeled cucumber. Slice cucumber; set aside. Rinse lettuce; drain (see photo 2, page 14). Line a 9-inch (23cm) pie tin with lettuce (see photo 4, page 15). Spoon potato salad atop lettuce in a ring around outside edge of pie tin. Place about *two-thirds* of the cucumber slices around edge. Drain salmon (see tip, page 21). Discard skin and bones. Break salmon into chunks, then place in centre. Arrange the remaining cucumber slices around salmon. Drain olives; scatter over salmon. Sprinkle with snipped fresh dill, if desired. Makes 4 servings.

Assembling time: 30 minutes

Hot Bread

Hot breads taste great with cold main-dish salads. Make breads special with a flavoured butter.

Consider serving a herb butter that you can keep on hand in the refrigerator: Stir ½ teaspoon dried *thyme,* crushed, and ½ teaspoon ground *sage* into ½ cup softened *butter.* Spread on slices of French bread. To heat the bread, stack slices, wrap in foil, and bake in a 350°F (180°c) gas mark 4 oven about 15 minutes.

Off-the-Shelf Recipes

Running late? Create delicious meals at a moment's notice with ingredients straight from your cupboard, freezer, and fridge shelves.

For example, we prepared this tempting and colourful Ham and Prawn Creole from easy, quick-to-use ingredients such as rice, tinned tomatoes and tomato puree, green peppers, frozen prawns, and cooked or tinned meat.

You'll be surprised at how many other recipes are waiting on your shelves. Turn to this chapter for more off-the-shelf main-dish ideas.

Ham and Prawn Creole

Ham and Prawn Creole

A little less than half a tin of ham makes a handy substitute for the cubed meat. See our tips for time-saving ideas.

10	ounces (275g) quick-cooking rice
1	ounce (25g) butter *or* margarine (optional)
16	ounces (450g) tinned tomatoes
6	ounces (175g) tomato puree
4	fluid ounces (110ml) water
3	ounces (75g) chopped green pepper
½	teaspoon dried thyme, crushed
½	teaspoon Worcestershire sauce
¼	teaspoon bottled hot pepper sauce
⅛	teaspoon garlic powder
6	ounces (175g) frozen cooked prawns
6	ounces (175g) ham
	Pickled okra (optional)

Cook rice according to packet directions. Stir in butter or margarine, if desired, then keep warm (see photo 1).

Meanwhile, cut up tomatoes (see photo 2). In a large saucepan stir together *undrained* tomatoes, tomato puree, water, green pepper, thyme, Worcestershire sauce, hot pepper sauce, and garlic powder. Bring to the boil. Reduce heat, then simmer, covered, for 20 minutes.

Meanwhile, thaw prawns (see photo 3). Drain and set prawns aside. Cut ham into ½-inch (1cm) cubes (see photo 4). Stir prawns and ham into tomato mixture. Simmer, uncovered, about 5 minutes more or until prawns and ham are heated through. Serve over rice. Garnish with pickled okra, if desired. Makes 4 servings.

Assembling time: 10 minutes
Cooking time: 25 minutes

1 Keep cooked rice warm in a covered saucepan. If you like, stir in an ounce (25g) of butter. It helps keep the rice grains from sticking together.

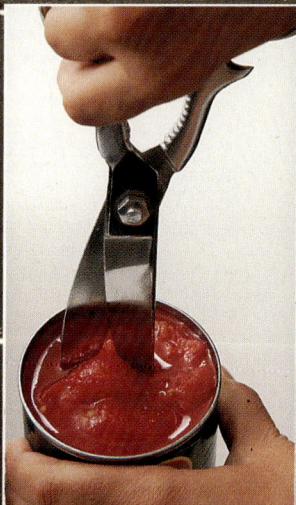

2 Save time by cutting up the large tomato pieces in the tin with kitchen scissors.

3 To thaw the frozen prawns, place them in a colander in your sink. Run warm tap water over the prawns for about 3 minutes or until thawed. You also can thaw frozen vegetables in a minute or two under warm running water.

4 Quickly cube or slice meat by lining up meat strips on a cutting board; cut crosswise all at once, as shown. For ½-inch (1cm) cubes, first cut a ½-inch thick (1cm) piece of meat into ½-inch (1cm) strips.

To eliminate a bowl, drain tinned foods—fish, meat, fruit—right in the tin. Using the lid, press against the food; invert to drain. Remove the lid. For meat or fish, break up with a fork, as shown. If you need to remove bones from the fish, drain the fish in the tin, then transfer the fish to a bowl.

Potato Shell Turkey Pie

2	ounces (50g) butter *or* margarine
4	fluid ounces (110ml) milk
8	ounces (225g) instant mashed potatoes
	Dash pepper
10	ounces (275g) frozen mixed vegetables
¾	pint (425ml) tinned leek and potato soup
2	ounces (50g) grated Swiss cheese
¼	teaspoon dried basil, crushed
10	ounces (275g) cooked turkey chunks
2	ounces (50g) prepared fried onions

In a medium saucepan melt butter or margarine. Stir in 4 fluid ounces (110ml) milk. Remove from heat, then stir in potatoes and pepper. Press potato mixture onto the bottom and up the sides of a greased 10-inch (25cm) pie plate.

Meanwhile, thaw frozen vegetables (see photo 3, page 20). In a mixing bowl stir together vegetables, soup, cheese, and basil.

Layer turkey atop potato crust. Top with soup mixture. Bake in a 350°F (180°C) gas mark 4 oven for 20 minutes. Sprinkle top with fried onions. Bake about 5 minutes more or until mixture is heated through. Makes 6 servings.

Assembling time: 20 minutes
Cooking time: 25 minutes

Tuna-Broccoli-Sauced Pastry

For an even faster version, spoon the tuna-broccoli mixture over cheese biscuits.

1	9-inch (23cm) folded frozen *or* refrigerated uncooked pastry
12	ounces (350g)) frozen cut broccoli
12	ounces (350g) tinned tuna
½	pint (275g) tinned condensed cream of celery soup
6	fluid ounces (165ml) milk
¾	teaspoon dried basil, crushed

Thaw pastry if necessary. Roll out to ⅛-inch (3mm) thick. With a pastry wheel or knife, cut uncooked pastry into 1-inch (2.5cm) pieces. Place pieces, in a single layer, on a greased baking tray. Bake in a 450°F (230°C) gas mark 8 oven for 7 to 8 minutes or until golden. Meanwhile, thaw broccoli (see photo 3, page 20). Set aside. Drain tuna and break into chunks (see tip, page 21). Set aside. In a medium saucepan stir together soup and milk; stir in broccoli, tuna, and basil. Cook over medium heat 12 to 15 minutes or until hot, stirring frequently. Spoon mixture over pastry pieces on dinner plates. Serves 6.

Assembling time: 15 minutes
Cooking time: 12 to 15 minutes

Quick Fruit Salads

Need a simple salad suggestion for dinner? Stir up a fruit combo—it's as easy as tossing greens with bottled dressing. Just put several cans of fruit in the refrigerator to chill. At meal time, drain and mix the fruit, then serve on lettuce-lined salad plates. The results are delicious and a welcome change from a tossed salad.

Seafood and Wild Rice Salad

If you already have crab or prawns in the freezer, use it in place of the tinned seafood.

- 9 ounces (250g) tinned prawns *or* 6½ ounces (185g) tinned crab
- 7 ounces (200g) quick-cooking long grain and wild rice mix
- 2 fluid ounces (55ml) red wine vinegar and oil salad dressing
- 2 ounces (50g) chopped green pepper, celery, *or* spring onion
- Lettuce leaves
- Tomato wedges (optional)
- Avocado slices (optional)

Place tinned prawns or crab in the freezer for 15 minutes to chill. Meanwhile, prepare long grain and wild rice mix according to packet directions. To chill rice quickly, place the saucepan in a large bowl or sink of ice water about 5 minutes or until cool, stirring occasionally (see photo 2, page 81).

Transfer rice to a bowl; stir in salad dressing and green pepper, celery, or spring onion. Cover and quick chill in the freezer 10 to 15 minutes. Drain seafood (see tip, page 21). Rinse tinned prawns or remove any cartilage from crab.

To assemble salads, line four chilled individual salad plates with lettuce. Spoon on a mound of rice mixture, then top with seafood. Arrange tomato wedges and avocado slices around rice mixture, if desired. Serve at once. Serves 4.

Total preparation time: 30 minutes

Chicken and Corkscrew Macaroni

If you don't have any corkscrew macaroni, plain macaroni works well, too.

- 6 ounces (175g) corkscrew *or* plain macaroni
- 8 ounces (225g) tinned tomatoes
- 15 ounces (425g) tinned sieved tomatoes
- 2 ounces (50g) chopped green pepper
- ½ teaspoon caster sugar
- ½ teaspoon dried Italian seasoning, crushed
- Dash pepper
- 10 ounces (275g) cooked chicken chunks
- 4 ounces (110g) grated mozzarella *or* Gouda cheese

Cook macaroni according to packet directions. Meanwhile, cut up tomatoes (see photo 2, page 20). In a large saucepan or 10-inch (25cm) frying pan stir together *undrained* tomatoes, sieved tomatoes, green pepper, sugar, Italian seasoning, and pepper. Bring the mixture to the boil. Reduce heat, then simmer, covered, for 10 minutes, stirring occasionally.

Drain macaroni. Stir drained macaroni and chicken into tomato mixture. Heat through. Transfer to a serving dish, then sprinkle with cheese. Makes 4 servings.

Assembling time: 10 minutes
Cooking time: 20 minutes

Easy Corned Beef Stroganoff

- 4 ounces (110g) wide *or* medium noodles
- 12 ounces (350g) tinned corned beef, chilled
- ¾ pint (425ml) beef *or* chicken stock
- 4 ounces (110g) tinned sliced mushrooms, drained
- 1 teaspoon minced dried onion
- 8 ounces (225g) soured cream
- 2 ounces (50g) plain flour
- 5 ounces (150g) frozen peas

Cook noodles according to packet directions; drain and keep warm (see photo 1, page 20). Meanwhile, remove corned beef from the tin and cut into ½-inch (1cm) cubes (see photo 4, page 21). Set aside.

In a saucepan stir together stock, mushrooms, and onion. Cook over medium heat until heated through. Stir together soured cream and flour. Stir soured cream mixture into mixture in saucepan. Bring to the boil, stirring constantly.

Stir corned beef cubes and peas into hot mixture. Cook about 5 minutes more or until peas are tender and meat is heated through. Serve over noodles. Makes 4 servings.

Total preparation time: 30 minutes

Sausage-Vegetable Stew

- 14 ounces (400g) tinned chopped tomatoes
- 1½ pounds (700g) sausages, cooked
- 2 tablespoons cornflour
- 1 tablespoon minced dried onion
- 1 teaspoon instant chicken bouillon granules
- ½ teaspoon dried basil, crushed
- 16 ounces (450g) tinned sliced carrots
- 4 fluid ounces (110ml) water
- 1 teaspoon Worcestershire sauce
- 16 ounces (450g) tinned potatoes
- 6 ounces (175g) packaged scone mix *or* 6 scones
- Sesame seed

Cut sausage into ½-inch-thick (1cm) slices (see photo 4, page 21). In a large saucepan stir together cornflour, onion, bouillon granules, and basil. Stir in *undrained* tomatoes, *undrained* carrots, water, and Worcestershire sauce. Cook and stir until thickened and bubbly.

Drain potatoes, then stir sausage and potatoes into mixture in saucepan. Cook until hot and bubbly. Meanwhile, if using packaged scone mix, prepare scone batter according to packet directions. Pour sausage mixture into a 2½-quart (2.75l) casserole. Quickly drop scone batter into six mounds atop *hot* mixture. (*Or,* quickly arrange scones over *hot* mixture.) Sprinkle sesame seed over scones. Bake in a 425°F (220°C) gas mark 7 oven for 12 to 15 minutes or until scones are golden brown. Serves 6.

Assembling time: 15 minutes
Cooking time: 12 to 15 minutes

◀ *Pictured opposite: Sausage-Vegetable Stew*

Hurry-Up Meat Loaves

How can you streamline the cooking time for a meat loaf? Form the meat into a ring or mini loaves—it'll bake faster that way. For even speedier results, use your microwave oven.

If you usually make meat loaf with minced beef, how about giving another type of meat a try and serving a lamb, ham, or pork loaf instead? We've got recipes for all of them on the following pages.

Pizza-Style Meat Loaf

Pizza-Style Meat Loaf

1	egg
8	fluid ounces (220ml) prepared pizza sauce
1½	ounces (40g) fine dry breadcrumbs
2	teaspoons minced dried onion
1	teaspoon dried oregano, crushed
¼	teaspoon pepper
1	pound (450g) minced beef
1	slice mozzarella cheese (1½ ounces, [40g])

In a bowl beat egg slightly. Stir in *4 fluid ounces (110ml)* of pizza sauce, crumbs, onion, oregano, and pepper. Add beef; mix well. Shape meat into a ring or mini loaves (see photos 1–3). Bake in a 350°F (180°C) gas mark 4 oven for 35 minutes. Spoon off fat (see photo 4).

Spoon remaining pizza sauce over meat. Bake about 5 minutes more or until meat is well done (see tip, page 30). Cut cheese into eight triangles. Arrange cheese atop meat. Bake about 1 minute more or until cheese begins to melt. Garnish with cherry tomatoes and parsley, if desired. Makes 4 servings.

Assembling time: 15 minutes
Cooking time: 41 minutes

Microwave Directions

Prepare meat mixture and shape into a ring in a non-metal pie plate (see photos 1 and 2). Cover and micro-cook on 100% power (HIGH) for 7 to 8 minutes or until done, turning dish (see tip, page 31). Spoon off fat (see photo 4).

Place remaining pizza sauce in a ½-pint (275ml) glass measure. Micro-cook, loosely covered, on 100% power (HIGH) for 30 to 45 seconds or until heated through, stirring once. Spoon sauce over meat. Arrange cheese on top of sauced meat. Let stand 5 minutes.

1 Mound the meat mixture in a pie plate. Shape it 2 inches (5cm) high and 5 inches (13cm) in diameter, as shown. Or, press meat into a 5-inch-diameter (13cm) bowl. Then, invert into a pie plate; remove bowl. Either way gives you the right shape.

2 Form a 2-inch-diameter (5cm) hole in the centre of the meat mound with your hands while maintaining the height of the loaf at 2 inches (5cm). The hole in the centre shortens baking time because heat can penetrate meat from all sides.

3 Another way to cut baking time is to make mini loaves. Form four 4x2-inch (10x5cm) loaves and then place them in a 10x6x2-inch (25x15x5cm) dish.

4 Spoon off any fat that bakes out of the meat loaf. Holding the dish with an oven glove, slightly tilt the baking dish to one side so it's easier to spoon off the dripping. Discard dripping.

Zesty Pork Loaves

1 egg
2 fluid ounces (55ml) buttermilk
3 ounces (75g) soft bread crumbs (2 slices)
4 ounces (110g) grated cheddar cheese
½ teaspoon salt
¼ teaspoon ground sage
⅛ teaspoon garlic powder
⅛ teaspoon dried basil, crushed
Dash pepper
1 pound (450g) minced pork

In a medium bowl beat egg slightly. Stir in buttermilk, crumbs, ¾ cup of cheese, salt, sage, garlic powder, basil, and pepper. Add pork, then mix well. Shape meat into four mini loaves (see photo 3, page 29). Bake mini loaves in a 350°F (180°C) gas mark 4 oven for 35 minutes. Spoon off fat (see photo 4, page 29). Sprinkle the loaves with remaining 1 ounce (25g) cheese. Bake about 5 minutes more or until meat is well done and cheese is melted (see tip below). Makes 4 servings.

Assembling time: 20 minutes
Cooking time: 40 minutes

Cook Them Well Done

Because minced meat gets handled more than other meats during processing, cook meat loaves until well done to ensure maximum food safety.

Follow the recipes timings. To be sure they're done, cut into the loaves to see that the inside colour of the meat is brown. Or, use a meat thermometer to check the cooked meat temperature—it should register 170°F (80°C).

Old-Fashioned Meat Loaf

Just like mother used to make, only this one uses speedy ingredients—dried onion and parsley.

1 egg
4 fluid ounces (110ml) milk
1½ ounces (40g) quick-cooking rolled oats
2 teaspoons minced dried onion
1 teaspoon dried parsley
½ teaspoon salt
⅛ teaspoon pepper
1 pound (450g) minced beef
4 tablespoons ketchup
½ teaspoon prepared mustard
½ teaspoon Worcestershire sauce

In a medium bowl beat egg slightly. Stir in milk, oats, onion, parsley, salt, and pepper. Add beef, then mix well. Shape meat into a ring (see photos 1 and 2, page 28).

Bake meat ring in a 350°F (180°C) gas mark 4 oven for 35 minutes. Spoon off fat (see photo 4, page 29). Combine ketchup, mustard, and Worcestershire sauce; spread over meat ring. Bake about 5 minutes more or until meat is well done (see tip at left). Makes 4 servings.

Assembling time: 15 minutes
Cooking time: 40 minutes

Microwave Directions: Prepare meat mixture and shape in a non-metal pie plate (see photos 1 and 2, page 28). Cover and microcook on 100% power (HIGH) for 8 to 9 minutes or until done, turning dish (see tip, page 31). Spoon off fat (see photo 4, page 29).

Combine topping mixture; spread over meat ring. Let stand, covered, for 5 minutes.

Individual Ham Loaves

2	eggs
1½	ounces (40g) fine dry breadcrumbs
2	tablespoons sliced spring onion
2	teaspoons French mustard
1	pound (450g) minced ham
10	ounces (275g) frozen peas
½	pint (275ml) prepared white sauce mix

In a medium bowl beat eggs slightly. Stir in crumbs, spring onion, and mustard. Add ham, then mix well. Shape meat into four mini loaves (see photo 3, page 29). Bake in a 350°F (180°C) gas mark 4 oven about 30 minutes. Meanwhile, prepare peas and white sauce mix according to packet directions. Mix together. Spoon over loaves. Makes 4 servings.

Assembling time: 15 minutes
Cooking time: 30 minutes

Microwave Directions: Prepare meat mixtures. Shape into mini loaves in a non-metal baking dish (see photo 3, page 29). Cover; micro-cook on 100% power (HIGH) 6 to 8 minutes or until done, turning dish (see tip below). Prepare peas and sauce; spoon over loaves.

Meat Loaf Microwave Tips

Choose shallow non-metal baking containers. Greaseproof paper or clingfilm makes a good cover for the meat during cooking. Give the baking dish a half-turn after 4 minutes of micro-cooking for more even cooking.

The microwave timings in this book were tested using countertop microwave ovens with 600 to 700 watts of cooking power. The cooking times are approximate because microwave ovens vary according to manufacturer.

Spinach and Lamb Loaf

Serving yogurt with this dish adds a cool tanginess.

10	ounces (275g) frozen chopped spinach, cooked
2	eggs
4	fluid ounces (110ml) milk
2	ounces (50g) fine dry breadcrumbs
1	ounce (25g) grated Parmesan cheese
½	teaspoon salt
½	teaspoon dried rosemary, crushed
¼	teaspoon onion powder
⅛	teaspoon pepper
1½	pounds (700g) minced lamb
	Natural yogurt

Drain spinach. In a medium bowl beat eggs slightly. Stir in spinach, milk, crumbs, cheese, salt, rosemary, onion powder, and pepper. Add lamb, then mix well. In a 10-inch (25.5cm) pie plate or 13x9x2-inch (32x23x5cm) baking tin, shape meat into a ring measuring 2 inches (5cm) high and 8 inches (20cm) in diameter (see photos 1 and 2, page 28).

Bake in a 350°F (180°C) gas mark 4 oven about 40 minutes or until the meat is well done (see tip, page 30). Spoon off the fat (see photo 4, page 29). Dollop the servings with yogurt. Makes 6 servings.

Assembling time: 25 minutes
Cooking time: 40 minutes

Microwave Directions: Prepare meat mixture and shape into a ring in a non-metal pie plate or pizza plate (see photos 1 and 2, page 28). Cover and micro-cook on 100% power (HIGH) for 12 to 14 minutes or until done, turning dish a quarter-turn every 4 minutes (see tip at left). Spoon off fat (see photo 4, page 29). Dollop with yogurt.

Speedy Frying Pan Suppers

Looking for a fix-it-fast recipe for supper? Search no further. We've created some tasty one-dish meals for you. Just pick one out and you're on your way to tonight's fuss-free supper.

Making and *serving* our supper dishes is so simple. You toss all the ingredients into a frying pan to cook. Then at meal time, take your frying pan to the table for serving. It's all so easy!

Mexicali Fry Up

Mexicali Fry Up

Save time! No need to cook the rice first—it cooks with other ingredients in this frying pan meal.

1	medium onion
1	tablespoon cooking oil
16	ounces (450g) tinned tomatoes
4	ounces (110g) green chilli peppers, diced
15	ounces (425g) tinned haricot *or* soya beans
8	fluid ounces (220ml) water
5	ounces (150g) long grain rice
1	teaspoon chilli powder
5	ounces (150g) chippolata sausages *or* 4 pork sausages, cooked and cut into 16 pieces
4	ounces (110g) grated cheddar cheese

Chop onion (see photo 1). In a 10-inch (25cm) frying pan cook onion in hot oil until tender but not brown (see photo 2). Cut up tomatoes. Drain chilli peppers. Add *undrained* tomatoes, chilli peppers, *undrained* beans, water, and *uncooked* rice to the frying pan (see photo 3). Stir in chilli powder. Bring to the boil (see photo 4). Reduce heat to medium-low, then simmer, covered, 15 minutes or until rice is nearly tender.

Stir rice mixture thoroughly. Arrange sausage pieces atop mixture (see photo 5). Simmer, covered, 5 minutes more or until sausages are heated through and rice is tender. Sprinkle cheese over mixture in the frying pan. Cover and cook about 2 minutes more or until cheese is almost melted. Makes 6 servings.

Assembling time: 15 minutes
Cooking time: 28 minutes

1 To chop onion, use a chef's knife to halve onion from top to root end. Place onion halves, flat side down, on a cutting board. Slice from top to bottom, making the cuts parallel. Then cut across the slices, as shown.

2 Cook and stir onion in hot oil until tender but not brown. The onion pieces will have a translucent appearance.

3 After adding the other ingredients to the frying pan, stir in uncooked rice. For these easy frying pan dishes, the juice from the vegetables, the broth, or the water that's added to the mixture is the cooking liquid for the rice, pasta, barley, or bulgur.

4 Bring the mixture to the boil over high heat, as shown. (Bubbles will rise to the surface and break.) Reduce heat to medium-low, cover, then continue simmering the mixture.

5 Stir rice mixture before placing the sausage pieces on top. Arrange sausages spoke-fashion, as shown, so that all the pieces fit on top of the mixture.

Salmon Stroganoff Frying Pan Supper

- 16 ounces (450g) tinned salmon
- 12 fluid ounces (330ml) vegetable juice cocktail
- 16 fluid ounces (440ml) strong chicken stock
- 3 ounces (75g) tinned sliced mushrooms
- 2 tablespoons snipped fresh parsley *or* 2 teaspoons dried parsley
- 2 teaspoons minced dried onion
- 1 teaspoon Worcestershire sauce
- ½ teaspoon dried basil, crushed
- ⅛ teaspoon pepper
- 5 ounces (150g) medium noodles
- 1 ounce (25g) plain flour
- 8 ounces (225g) soured cream

Drain salmon (see tip, page 21). Discard skin and bones, then flake fish. Set aside.

In a 10-inch (25cm) frying pan stir together vegetable juice cocktail, stock, *undrained* mushrooms, parsley, onion, Worcestershire sauce, basil, and pepper. Stir in *uncooked* noodles (see photo 3, page 34). Bring mixture to the boil (see photo 4, page 35). Reduce heat to medium-low, then simmer, covered, for 12 to 15 minutes or until noodles are tender, stirring once or twice.

Thoroughly stir flour into soured cream, then stir into mixture in the frying pan. Cook and stir over medium-high heat until thickened and bubbly, then cook and stir 1 minute more. Stir in salmon, then heat through. Makes 6 servings.

Assembling time: 20 minutes
Cooking time: 22 to 25 minutes

Chicken and Bulgur Frying Pan Supper

Bulgur is precooked cracked wheat.

- 1 medium onion
- 1 ounce (25g) butter *or* margarine
- ¾ pint (425ml) chicken stock
- 8 ounces (225g) broccoli florets *or* 10 ounces (275g) frozen broccoli florets
- 6 ounces (175g) diced cooked chicken
- 3 ounces (75g) bulgur wheat
- ¼ teaspoon garlic powder

Cut onion into thin wedges. In a 10-inch (25cm) frying pan cook onion in hot butter or margarine over low heat until onion is tender but not brown (see photo 2, page 34). Stir occasionally.

Add broth, broccoli, chicken, bulgur, and garlic powder to the frying pan (see photo 3, page 34). Bring mixture to the boil (see photo 4, page 35.) Break up block of frozen broccoli, if used, with a fork. Reduce heat, then simmer, covered, 10 to 12 minutes or until bulgur and broccoli are done. Makes 4 servings.

Assembling time: 10 minutes
Cooking time: 16 to 18 minutes

Freezer-to-Table Frying Pan Supper

Keep the major ingredients—chicken, vegetables, and rice—on hand in your freezer for this delightful dish.

8	frozen chicken legs *or* thighs*
½	small onion
2	fluid ounces (55ml) water
3	tablespoons teriyaki sauce *or* soy sauce
8	ounces (225g) frozen cut green beans
6	ounces (175g) frozen crinkle-cut carrots
20	ounces (550g) cooked long grain rice
2	tablespoons slivered almonds

Run warm water over frozen chicken and tap lightly on countertop to separate pieces. Chop onion (see photo 1, page 34). In a 12-inch (30cm) frying pan combine onion, water, and teriyaki or soy sauce. Add the frozen chicken. Bring mixture to the boil. Reduce heat, then simmer, covered, about 30 minutes or until chicken is almost tender.

Meanwhile, place beans and carrots in a colander. Run warm water over vegetables until separated (see photo 3, page 20). Add vegetables and rice to chicken in the frying pan.

Bring mixture to the boil (see photo 4, page 35). Reduce heat, then simmer, covered, for 10 to 15 minutes more or until chicken and vegetables are tender, stirring once or twice to break up rice. Sprinkle almonds on top. Serves 4.

***Note:** If you freeze the chicken pieces separately, they'll be easier to work with. Or, start with fresh chicken pieces. Reduce the cooking time to just 20 minutes before adding the rice and vegetables.

Total preparation time: 60 to 65 minutes

Macaroni-Beef Supper

The chow mein noodles add the crunch to this main-dish-in-a-frying-pan.

1	pound (450g) minced beef
16	ounces (450g) tinned cut green beans, drained
12	fluid ounces (330ml) water
8	fluid ounces (220ml) tinned condensed cream of mushroom soup
2	teaspoons instant beef bouillon granules
1	teaspoon minced dried onion
1	teaspoon Worcestershire sauce
¼	teaspoon salt
	Dash garlic powder
	Dash pepper
3	ounces (75g) tiny shell macaroni
3	ounces (75g) cream cheese, cubed
3	ounces (75g) tinned chow mein noodles

In a 10-inch (25.5cm) frying pan cook beef till brown. Drain off fat. Stir in beans, water, soup, bouillon granules, onion, Worcestershire sauce, salt, garlic powder, and pepper. Stir in *uncooked* macaroni (see photo 3, page 34).

Bring to the boil (see photo 4, page 35). Reduce heat to medium-low, then simmer, covered, 20 to 25 minutes or until macaroni is tender, stirring once or twice. Stir in cream cheese cubes. Heat and stir until cheese is melted. Sprinkle with chow mein noodles. Makes 4 servings.

Assembling time: 10 minutes
Cooking time: 25 to 30 minutes

Rush Hour Simmer Dinner

Nested vermicelli is an unusually shaped pasta that's been dried in a little bundle resembling a bird's nest. Look for it in the pasta section of your supermarket. To serve, give each person a bundle.

1	medium onion
1	tablespoon cooking oil
4	bundles nested vermicelli (about 5 ounces [150g] each)
¾	pint (420ml) chicken stock
1	teaspoon dried tarragon, crushed
5	ounces (150g) frozen peas
5	ounces (150g) frozen carrots
14	ounces (400g) chopped cooked chicken

Slice onion. In a 10-inch (25.5cm) frying pan cook onion in hot oil until tender but not brown (see photo 2, page 34). Place *uncooked* vermicelli nests in the frying pan. Combine chicken stock and tarragon; carefully pour into the frying pan. Add peas and carrots; break up. Bring to the boil (see photo 4, page 35). Reduce heat to medium-low, then simmer, covered, for 15 minutes.

Add chicken; simmer, covered, 5 to 10 minutes more or until pasta is tender and chicken is hot. Makes 4 servings.

Assembling time: 10 minutes
Cooking time: 25 to 30 minutes

Tuna-Spaghetti Frying Pan Supper

Cook spaghetti in a herbed soup mixture until the pasta is al dente—tender but still slightly firm.

1	medium onion
1	tablespoon cooking oil
1¼	pints (600ml) tinned leek and potato soup
4	ounces (110g) spaghetti, broken
½	teaspoon dried savory, crushed
10	ounces (275g) frozen broccoli florets
9	ounces (250g) tinned tuna
2½	ounces (60g) tinned sliced mushrooms, drained
2	tablespoons grated Parmesan cheese

Chop onion (see photo 1, page 34). In a 10-inch (25.5cm) frying pan cook onion in hot oil until tender but not brown (see photo 2, page 34). Add soup and *uncooked* spaghetti to the frying pan (see photo 3, page 34). Stir in savory. Bring mixture to the boil (see photo 4, page 35). Reduce heat to medium-low, then simmer, covered, for 15 minutes.

Meanwhile, run warm water over broccoli to break up (see photo 3, page 20). Drain, chop, and set aside. Drain and flake tuna (see tip, page 21). Gently stir broccoli, tuna, and mushrooms into frying pan. Cook, covered, for 5 to 10 minutes more or until spaghetti is done. Sprinkle with Parmesan cheese. Makes 4 servings.

Assembling time: 10 minutes
Cooking time: 25 to 30 minutes

Ham and Spaetzle Frying Pan Supper

Spaetzle (SHPETS luh) is a dumpling that has an irregular shape. Buy the spaetzle at the supermarket.

- 1 medium onion
- 1 tablespoon cooking oil
- ½ pound (225g) cubed ham
- 10¾ fluid ounces (280ml) tinned condensed cream of celery soup
- 8 ounces (225g) packet frozen cut green beans
- 6 ounces (175g) dried spaetzle *or* small egg noodles
- 8 fluid ounces (220ml) water
- ¾ teaspoon caraway seed

Chop onion (see photo 1, page 34). In a 10-inch (25cm) frying pan cook onion in hot oil until tender but not brown (see photo 2, page 34). Add ham, soup, beans, *uncooked* spaetzle, water, and caraway seed to the frying pan (see photo 3, page 34).

Bring to the boil (see photo 4, page 35). Reduce heat to medium-low, then simmer, covered, for 20 minutes. Stir occasionally to prevent sticking. Remove from heat and let stand, covered, 5 minutes. Makes 4 servings.

Assembling time: 10 minutes
Cooking time: 25 minutes
Standing time: 5 minutes

Barley-Sausage Frying Pan Supper

- 1 medium onion
- 1 large carrot
- 1 tablespoon cooking oil
- 16 ounces (450g) tinned sauerkraut, rinsed, drained, and snipped
- ¾ pint (425ml) beef stock
- 12 ounces (350g) cooked German sausage, cut into 1-inch (2cm) pieces
- 4 ounces (110g) quick-cooking barley
- 2 fluid ounces (55ml) water
- ½ teaspoon dried basil, crushed
- 2 ounces (50g) grated cheddar cheese

Chop onion (see photo 1, page 34). Grate carrot. In a 10-inch (25cm) frying pan cook onion and carrot in hot oil until tender but not brown (see photo 2, page 34). Add sauerkraut, beef broth, sausage, *uncooked* barley, water, and basil to frying pan (see photo 3, page 34). Bring to the boil (see photo 4, page 35). Reduce heat to medium-low, then simmer, covered, for 15 to 20 minutes or until barley is done.

Sprinkle cheese over mixture in the frying pan. Cover and let stand 1 to 2 minutes more or until cheese melts. Makes 4 servings.

Assembling time: 15 minutes
Cooking time: 20 to 25 minutes
Standing time: 1 to 2 minutes

Streamlined Soups

You can forget the idea that delicious homemade soups take hours to cook—our recipes don't. They're all hearty main dishes that are ready in 40 minutes or less.

While the soup cooks, arrange some breadsticks, water biscuits, or crispy French bread in a basket, and you've got a "souper" quick meal ready to enjoy.

Fish Chowder

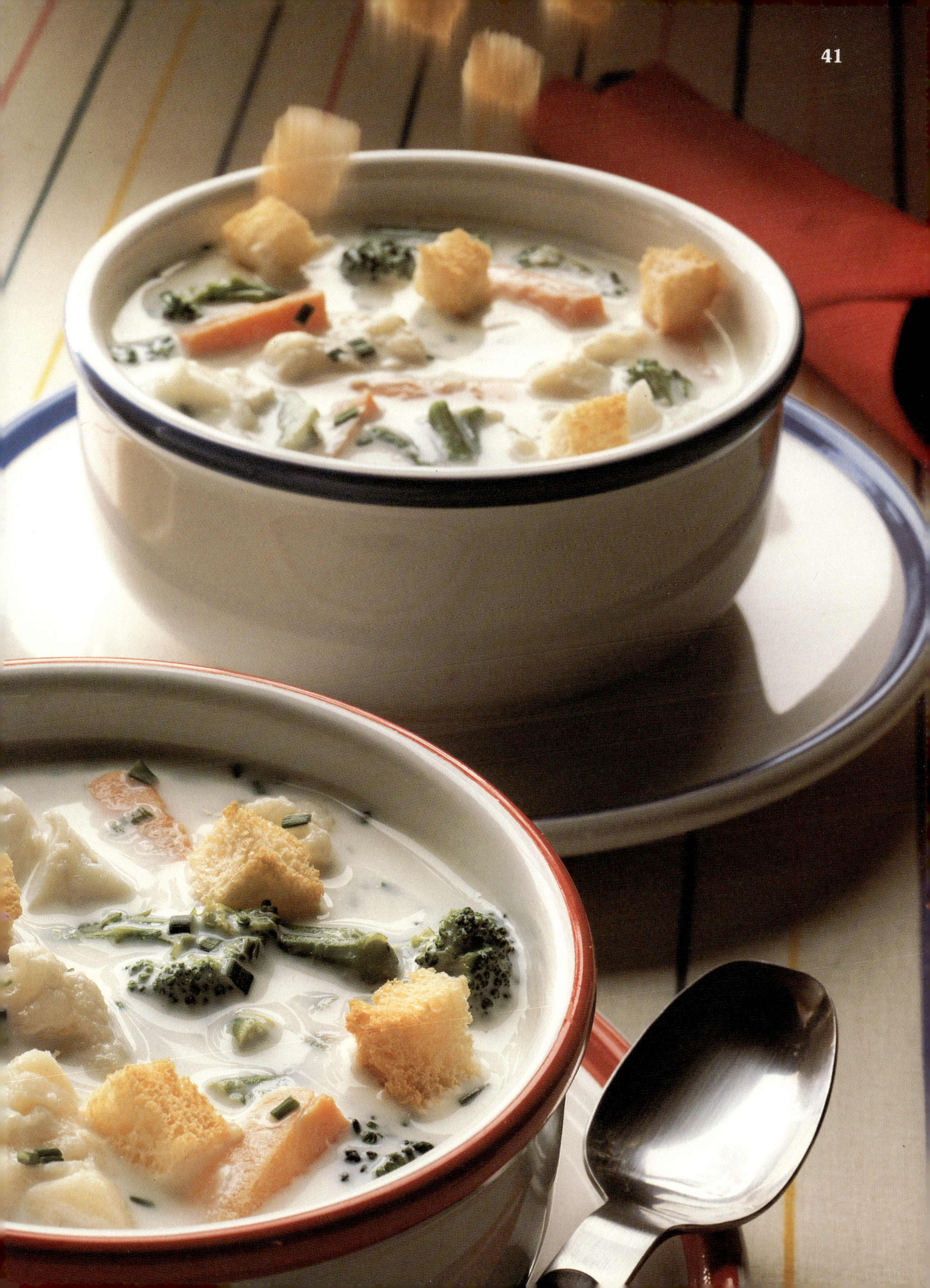

Fish Chowder

No need to buy and prepare several vegetables for this chowder. Just use a convenient frozen mixture.

- 1 pound (450g) fresh *or* frozen fish fillets
- 16 ounces (450g) loose-pack frozen mixed cauliflower, broccoli, and carrots
- 1¼ pints (720ml) milk
- 4 tablespoons snipped chives
- ⅛ teaspoon salt
- ⅛ teaspoon pepper
- ¾ pint (425ml) single cream
- 1½ ounces (40g) plain flour
- ¼ teaspoon ground nutmeg (optional)
- Plain croutons (optional)

If frozen, thaw fish at room temperature 20 minutes. Meanwhile, cut up large pieces of frozen vegetables, then add to a 6½-pint (3.7l) casserole (see photo 1). Add milk, chives, salt, and pepper to the casserole. Cook the milk-vegetable mixture over medium-high heat, stirring occasionally, just until it boils.

Shake *4 fluid ounces (110ml)* of the cream and flour together (see photo 2). Stir flour mixture into hot milk-vegetable mixture in the casserole (see photo 3). Add remaining cream. Cook and stir until thickened and bubbly (see photo 4).

With a heavy knife, cut fish into 1-inch (2.5cm) pieces (see photo 5). Add fish and nutmeg, if desired, to soup mixture. Cook, stirring occasionally, 5 to 10 minutes more or until fish flakes easily with a fork. Season to taste with salt, if desired. Ladle mixture into soup bowls. Sprinkle with croutons, if desired. Makes 6 servings.

Total preparation time: 35 to 40 minutes

1 To ensure even cooking, cut up any large pieces of the frozen vegetables before adding them to the casserole. Then, add vegetables along with milk, chives, salt, and pepper to the casserole.

3 Gradually pour the flour-cream mixture into the casserole with hot milk-vegetable mixture. Be sure to stir constantly while pouring to prevent chowder from becoming lumpy.

2 Shake flour and part of the cream together in a jar with a screw-top lid, as shown. Shake vigorously to completely combine flour with cream.

If you don't have a screw-top jar, use another container with a lid; be sure to keep your finger on the lid while shaking so the cover doesn't come off.

4 Cook and stir until thickened and bubbly. Stir constantly to prevent mixture from sticking to the bottom of the pan. When thickened, the mixture will coat a spoon, as shown.

5 Use a heavy knife to cut the fresh or partially thawed fish into 1-inch (2.5cm) pieces.

Bratwurst-Potato Chowder

An unusual but delicious way to use a packaged scalloped potato mix.

1¼ pints (720ml) water
2 3-ounce (75g) packets dry scalloped potato mix
10 ounces (275g) frozen mixed vegetables
12 ounces (350g) cooked bratwurst
32 fluid ounces (900ml) milk
3 tablespoons plain flour
¼ teaspoon salt

In a 6½-pint (3.7l) casserole combine water, potatoes from mix (reserve seasoning packet), and vegetables. Bring mixture to the boil. Reduce heat, then simmer, covered, for 15 minutes, stirring occasionally.

Cut bratwurst into thin slices. Stir bratwurst and *28 fluid ounces (790ml)* of milk into hot soup mixture in the casserole. Shake remaining 4 fluid ounces (110ml) milk, flour, salt, and seasoning packet from potato mix together (see photo 2, page 43).

Stir flour mixture into soup (see photo 3, page 43). Cook and stir until thickened and bubbly (see photo 4, page 43). Cook and stir 1 minute more. Makes 6 servings.

Total preparation time: 25 minutes

Beer-Cheese Soup

This hearty soup boasts a wonderfully rich, full-bodied cheese flavour.

1 pint (570ml) water
8 fluid ounces (220ml) beer
3 ounces (75g) small shell macaroni
½ teaspoon instant chicken bouillon granules
½ teaspoon minced dried onion
½ teaspoon dried basil, crushed
 Several dashes bottled hot pepper sauce
2 fluid ounces (55ml) cold water
2 tablespoons plain flour
8 ounces (225g) grated mild cheddar cheese

In a large saucepan combine 1 pint (570ml) water, beer, *uncooked* macaroni, bouillon granules, onion, basil, and hot pepper sauce. Bring to the boil. Reduce heat, then simmer, uncovered, for 10 minutes, stirring occasionally.

Shake 2 fluid ounces (55ml) water and flour together (see photo 2, page 43). Stir flour mixture into hot mixture in the saucepan (see photo 3, page 43). Cook and stir until thickened and bubbly (see photo 4, page 43). Cook and stir 1 minute more. Stir in cheese. Heat and stir until cheese is melted. Makes 4 servings.

Assembling time: 5 minutes
Cooking time: 20 minutes

Savoury Beef-Vegetable Soup

Mixed vegetables add the colour to this herb-seasoned soup. You even have a choice of herbs!

¾	pound (350g) minced beef
¾	pint (425ml) beef stock
8	ounces frozen mixed vegetables
¾	teaspoon dried basil *or* oregano, crushed
⅛	teaspoon pepper
12	fluid ounces (330ml) vegetable juice cocktail
4	fluid ounces (110ml) cold water
2	tablespoons plain flour

In a large saucepan coarsely crumble minced beef, then cook until brown. Drain off fat. Add broth, vegetables with sauce, basil or oregano, and pepper; mix well. Bring to the boil. Reduce heat, then simmer, covered, for 10 minutes. Stir in the vegetable juice cocktail.

Shake water and flour together (see photo 2, page 43). Stir flour mixture into hot mixture in the saucepan (see photo 3, page 43). Cook and stir until mixture is slightly thickened and is bubbly (see photo 4, page 43). Cook and stir 1 minute more. Makes 4 servings.

Assembling time: 5 minutes
Cooking time: 20 minutes

Herbed Broccoli Soup

Need a recipe for leftover chicken or ham? Here's one with a delicate Swiss cheese flavour.

¾	pint (425ml) chicken stock
4	ounces (110g) finely chopped onion
¼	teaspoon dried thyme, crushed
10	ounces frozen broccoli, chopped
6	fluid ounces (165ml) milk
1½	ounces (40g) plain flour
½	pint (275ml) milk
8	ounces (225g) chopped cooked chicken, turkey, *or* ham
2	ounces (50g) grated Swiss cheese

In a large saucepan combine stock, onion, and thyme. Add broccoli. Bring to the boil. Reduce heat, then simmer, covered, for 5 minutes.

Shake 6 fluid ounces (165ml) milk and flour together (see photo 2, page 43). Stir flour mixture into hot stock-vegetable mixture in the saucepan (see photo 3, page 43). Add remaining ½ pint (275ml) milk. Cook and stir until thickened and bubbly (see photo 4, page 43). Cook and stir 1 minute more. Stir in chicken, turkey, or ham and grated cheese. Heat and stir until meat is heated through and cheese is melted. Makes 4 servings.

Assembling time: 20 minutes
Cooking time: 15 minutes

No-Fuss Oven-Frying

Our speedy solution for easy frying cuts down on kitchen duty. Put these recipes together in minutes and then leave them alone to cook in the oven. You'll get the flavour of deep-fat frying—without the mess.

We've even simplified your clearing up. Put the coating mixture into a polythene bag; add meat, shake to coat, and bake. Just toss out the messy coating bag when you've finished.

Oven-Fried Chicken

Oven-Fried Chicken

You'll need two polythene bags for the coating mixtures in this recipe.

- 1½ ounces (40g) plain flour
- ½ teaspoon dried savory
- ½ teaspoon dried thyme
- ¼ teaspoon salt
- 3 ounces (75g) cornflakes
- 2 tablespoons sesame seed
- 1 egg
- 2 fluid ounces (55ml) milk
- 1 2½- to 3-pound (1kg125g to 1kg350g) chicken, cut up

In a polythene bag combine flour, savory, thyme, and salt, then mix well. In another bag coarsely crush cornflakes (see photo 1). Add sesame seed to cereal, then mix well. In a shallow mixing bowl beat egg slightly with a fork, then stir in milk.

Split chicken breast (see photo 2). Cut chicken legs and thighs apart (see photo 3). Rinse chicken, then pat dry with kitchen paper. Place two or three chicken pieces at a time into bag with flour mixture. Shake well to coat. Dip floured chicken into egg-milk mixture. Coat with crushed cereal mixture (see photo 4).

Place the chicken pieces, skin side up and pieces not touching, on a greased 15x10x1-inch (38x25x2cm) baking tray. Repeat with remaining chicken. Bake, uncovered, in a 375°F (190°C) gas mark 5 oven for 40 to 50 minutes or until chicken is easily pierced with a fork. *Do not turn.* Makes 6 servings.

Assembling time: 20 minutes
Cooking time: 40 to 50 minutes

1 Place cereal in a large polythene bag. Loosely close bag by folding over end, leaving some room in the bag. Use a rolling pin or crush cereal with your hands. You'll get about half as many crushed crumbs as the original measure of cereal.

2 Store-packaged, cut-up chicken often needs additional cutting. Split the whole chicken breast into two lengthwise pieces through the breastbone. Use a large sharp knife.

3 To split the leg and thigh into two separate pieces, locate the knee joint. Do this by bending the thigh and leg together. Place chicken on a cutting board and cut through the joint.

4 Add the floured and egg-dipped chicken pieces to the bag containing the crumbs mixed with the sesame seed. By adding only a piece or two at a time, each piece gets evenly coated. Roll or gently shake the pieces in the crumb mixture, pressing the crumbs onto the chicken to coat evenly.

Italian-Seasoned Chicken Thighs

- 1 ounce (25g) butter *or* margarine
- 15 small round salted crackers
- 1 teaspoon dried Italian seasoning, crushed
- 6 chicken thighs

Preheat oven to 375°F (190°C) gas mark 5 for 10 minutes. In a 12x7½x2-inch (30x19x5cm) baking dish heat butter or margarine 5 minutes. Meanwhile, in a polythene bag coarsely crush crackers (see photo 1, page 48). Add Italian seasoning to crumbs, then mix well.

Place chicken in baking dish; turn once to coat surfaces of chicken with butter. Coat chicken with crumb mixture (see photo 4, page 49). Return chicken to baking dish. Bake, uncovered, in 375°F (190°C) gas mark 5 oven for 45 to 50 minutes or until chicken is easily pierced with a fork. *Do not turn.* Makes 3 servings.

Assembling time: 20 minutes
Cooking time: 45 to 50 minutes

Homemade Convenience

Grating and chopping in double (or more) batches makes good sense. You'll have ingredients ready to use when you need them.

When using the grater, grate enough cheese for two recipes, instead of one. Tightly wrap the extras; store in the refrigerator.

Or, chop extras when using your chopping board and chef's knife. Onions, green pepper, or nuts are commonly used ingredients that can be chopped in quantity. Chill or freeze them for future use.

Herbed Breaded Pork Chops

Mushroom soup serves a dual purpose—it adds flavour and helps the coating mixture cling to the chops.

- 3 ounces (75g) country stuffing mix
- ¼ teaspoon ground red pepper
- 1 ounce (25g) butter *or* margarine, melted and cooled
- 8 fluid ounces (220ml) condensed cream of mushroom soup
- 6 pork chops, cut ¾ inch (2cm) thick and trimmed of separable fat

In a polythene bag combine stuffing mix and red pepper, then mix well. Drizzle butter or margarine over mixture in bag, then mix well.

Pour soup into a shallow mixing bowl. Dip pork chop into condensed soup. Coat with crumb mixture (see photo 4, page 49). Place coated pork chop on an ungreased 15x10x1-inch (38x25x2cm) baking tray.

Repeat with remaining pork chops. Bake, uncovered, in a 375°F (190°C) gas mark 5 oven for 45 to 50 minutes or until chops are no longer pink. Makes 6 servings.

Assembling time: 10 minutes
Cooking time: 45 to 50 minutes

Veal Parmigiano

Use prepared pizza sauce for a quick meat sauce.

1½ ounces (40g) butter *or* margarine
2 ounces (50g) fine dry breadcrumbs
1 ounce (25g) grated Parmesan cheese
⅛ teaspoon salt
1 egg
1 tablespoon milk
¾ pound (350g) veal fillet or escalopes, cut ¼ inch thick
8 fluid ounces (220ml) prepared pizza sauce
2 slices mozzarella cheese, halved (3 ounces [75g])

Preheat oven to 400°F (200°C) gas mark 6 for 10 minutes. On a 13x9x2-inch (32x23x5cm) baking tray heat butter or margarine 5 minutes.

Meanwhile, in a polythene bag combine crumbs, Parmesan cheese, and salt, then mix well. In a shallow mixing bowl beat egg slightly with a fork, then stir in milk. Cut veal into four pieces. Dip one piece of veal into egg-milk mixture. Place in the bag with crumb mixture (see photo 4, page 49). Shake gently to coat all sides.

Place veal on the baking tray atop melted butter. Repeat with remaining veal. Bake, uncovered, in the 400°F (200°C) gas mark 6 oven for 10 minutes. Turn veal over. Spoon pizza sauce over veal. Bake about 15 minutes more or until meat is tender. Top with mozzarella cheese. Bake 1 to 2 minutes more or just until cheese melts. Makes 4 servings.

Assembling time: 15 minutes
Cooking time: 27 minutes

Oven-Fried Fish

Select your favourite variety of fish.

1 pound (450g) frozen fish fillets
1 ounce (25g) butter *or* margarine
2 ounces (50g) fine dry breadcrumbs
½ teaspoon paprika
¼ teaspoon celery salt *or* onion salt
1 egg
Tartar sauce (optional)

Thaw frozen fish at room temperature for 20 minutes. Meanwhile, preheat oven to 450°F (230°C) gas mark 8 for 10 minutes. On an 11x7x1½-inch (28x18x4cm) baking tray heat butter or margarine 5 minutes. In a polythene bag combine crumbs, paprika, and celery or onion salt, then mix well.

Use a sharp knife to cut the block of fish into eight equal portions; pat fish dry. In a shallow mixing bowl beat egg slightly with a fork. Dip one fish portion into beaten egg. Place into the bag with crumb mixture (see photo 4, page 49). Shake gently to evenly coat.

Place fish piece on the baking tray atop melted butter. Repeat with remaining fish. Bake, uncovered, in the 450°F (230°C) gas mark 8 oven for 25 to 30 minutes or until fish flakes easily with a fork. Serve fish with tartar sauce, if desired. Makes 4 servings.

Assembling time: 30 minutes
Cooking time: 25 to 30 minutes

Slow Cooker Meals

For a more relaxed dinnertime, fix most of your evening meal early in the day. How? Use an electric slow cooker.

Meat and vegetables slowly simmer on their own, developing a savoury blend of flavours. The results of trouble-free cooking? A deliciously hearty meal that's practically ready to set on the table when your appetite says "Let's eat!"

Barbecue-Style Pork Roast

Barbecue-Style Pork Roast

- 2 large green peppers
- 1 large onion
- 2 sticks celery
- 8 ounces (225g) tinned tomatoes
- 2½ to 3 pound (1.2 to 1.4kg) boneless pork shoulder
- 4 fluid ounces (110ml) bottled barbecue sauce
- 2 fluid ounces (55ml) dry red wine
- ½ teaspoon ground cumin
- 2 tablespoons cornflour
- 2 tablespoons cold water

Thinly cut green peppers into strips and onion into slices. Chop celery. Cut up tomatoes (see photo 2, page 20). In a 3-quart (3.5l) electric slow cooker place green peppers, onion, and celery (see photo 1). Add *undrained* tomatoes. Trim excess fat from pork, then cut joint to fit the slow cooker (see photo 2). Place meat on top of vegetables (see photo 3).

In a bowl stir together barbecue sauce, wine, and cumin, then pour over roast. Cover the cooker. Cook on low-heat setting for 9 to 10 hours or until meat and vegetables are tender.

To serve, transfer meat and vegetables to a serving plate and keep warm. Pour liquid into a large glass measure (see photo 4). Skim fat from cooking liquid (see photo 5). Measure ¾ pint (425ml) cooking liquid; add water, if necessary, to make ¾ pint (425ml) liquid.

For sauce, in a small saucepan stir together cornflour and water. Stir in ¾ pint (425ml) reserved cooking liquid. Cook and stir until thickened and bubbly, then cook and stir 2 minutes more. Pour sauce over meat and vegetables. Makes 6 servings.

Assembling time: 15 minutes
Cooking time: 9 to 10 hours
Final preparation time: 10 minutes

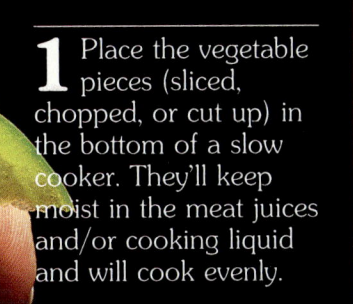

1 Place the vegetable pieces (sliced, chopped, or cut up) in the bottom of a slow cooker. They'll keep moist in the meat juices and/or cooking liquid and will cook evenly.

2 If necessary, cut the joint to fit the size of the cooker you are using. A handy cutting guide is the lid of your slow cooker.

3 Arrange the pieces of meat atop the vegetables in the slow cooker.

4 For gravy or sauce, remove meat and vegetables from cooker using a meat fork and a slotted spoon or fish slice. Transfer to a serving dish then cover with foil to keep warm. Pour cooking liquid into a glass measuring jug.

5 Skim fat from the cooking liquid using a spoon. Tip the measure slightly to dip off all the fat; try not to dip off any of the meat drippings.

Turkey Roast with Sweet Potatoes

Reserve half of the turkey for leftovers. One recipe suggestion for leftover turkey is Herbed Broccoli Soup on page 45.

- 3 to 3½ pound (1.4 to 1.6kg) frozen boneless turkey
- 6 fluid ounces (165ml) apple juice concentrate
- 3 large sweet potatoes (8 ounces [225g] each)
- 3 inches stick cinnamon
- ¼ teaspoon whole cloves
- 2 fluid ounces (55ml) water
- 2 tablespoons cornflour
- 2 tablespoons cold water

Thaw turkey according to directions. Peel potatoes and cut in half lengthwise. In a 3-quart (3.5l) electric slow cooker place potatoes (see photo 1, page 55). Add cinnamon and cloves to the cooker. Place turkey on top of potatoes in the slow cooker (see photo 3, page 55).

Combine apple juice concentrate and 2 fluid ounces (55ml) water, then pour into the slow cooker. Cover the cooker. Cook on low-heat setting for 9 to 11 hours or until the internal temperature of turkey is 185°F (90°C).

To serve, transfer turkey and potatoes to a serving plate; keep warm. Strain juices and pour into a large glass measure (see photo 4, page 55). Skim fat from juices (see photo 5, page 55). Measure ¾ pint (425ml) juices; add water if necessary. For sauce, in a small saucepan stir together cornflour and 2 tablespoons cold water. Stir in ¾ pint (425ml) reserved juices. Cook and stir until thickened and bubbly; cook and stir 2 minutes more. Season to taste with salt and pepper. Pass sauce. Makes 6 to 8 servings.

Assembling time: thawing time plus 20 minutes
Cooking time: 9 to 11 hours
Final preparation time: 10 minutes

Sweet 'n' Sour Chicken Dinner

Puzzled about which chicken pieces are meatiest? They're the breast portions, thighs, and legs.

- 6 medium carrots, peeled and cut into ¼-inch (.5cm) slices
- 1 large green pepper, seeded and cut into 1-inch (2.5cm) squares
- 1 medium onion, cut into wedges
- 3 whole medium chicken breasts, split lengthwise, *or* 2½ to 3 pounds (1.2 to 1.4kg) meaty chicken pieces
- ¼ teaspoon salt
- 16 ounces (450g) tinned pineapple chunks, drained
- 8 fluid ounces (220ml) sweet-sour sauce
- 2 tablespoons cornflour
- 2 tablespoons cold water
- Hot cooked rice

In a 3-quart (3.5l) electric slow cooker place carrots, green pepper, and onion (see photo 1, page 55). Place chicken atop vegetables in the cooker (see photo 3, page 55). Sprinkle with salt. Pour pineapple and sweet-sour sauce over chicken. Cover the cooker. Cook chicken and vegetables on low-heat setting for 8 to 9 hours or until tender.

To serve, transfer chicken, pineapple, and vegetables to a serving plate and keep warm. Pour juices into a large glass measure (see photo 4, page 55). Skim fat from juices (see photo 5, page 55). Measure ¾ pint (425ml) juices.

For sauce, in a small saucepan stir together cornflour and water. Stir in ¾ pint (425ml) reserved juices. Cook and stir until thickened and bubbly, then cook and stir 2 minutes more. Spoon over chicken mixture. Serve with rice. Makes 6 servings.

Assembling time: 25 minutes
Cooking time: 8 to 9 hours
Final preparation time: 10 minutes

German-Style Pot Roast

- 6 small potatoes (about 1 pound [450g])
- 4 to 6 medium carrots
- 1 medium onion, cut into ¼-inch (.5cm) slices
- 3 pounds (1.35kg) topside of beef
- 2 fluid ounces (55ml) vinegar
- 2 fluid ounces (55ml) water
- 2 bay leaves
- ½ teaspoon instant beef bouillon granules
- ¼ teaspoon ground cloves
- ⅛ teaspoon garlic powder
- Cooking oil (optional)
- 4 gingernuts, crushed

Scrub potatoes. Cut carrots into 2-inch (5cm) pieces. In a 3-quart (3.5l) electric slow cooker place vegetables (see photo 1, page 55). If necessary, cut meat in half to fit the cooker (see photo 2, page 55). Place meat atop vegetables (see photo 3, page 55).

Stir together vinegar, water, bay leaves, bouillon granules, cloves, garlic powder, and ½ teaspoon *salt*. Pour over meat in the cooker. For a moister top, brush surface of meat with a little oil. Cover the cooker. Cook on low-heat setting for 9 to 11 hours or until meat is tender.

To serve, transfer meat and vegetables to a serving plate and keep warm. Remove bay leaves. Pour juices into a large glass measure (see photo 4, page 55). Skim fat from juices (see photo 5, page 55). Measure 12 fluid ounces (330ml) juices; add additional water if necessary. For gravy, pour juices into a small saucepan. Stir gingernut crumbs into pan juices. Cook and stir until thickened and bubbly, then cook and stir 1 minute more. Slice meat. Pass gravy separately. Makes 6 servings.

Assembling time: 15 minutes
Cooking time: 9 to 11 hours
Final preparation time: 10 minutes

Beef Sandwiches: Shred leftover beef using two forks; discard fat and bones. For each 1 cup of beef, heat with 3 tablespoons bottled *barbecue sauce*. Serve on *baps* with *spinach* or *lettuce leaves*.

Corned Beef and Brussels Sprouts

The sprouts replace cabbage in this old-fashioned dish.

- 6 small potatoes
- 3 medium parsnips *or* carrots
- 10 ounces (275g) frozen brussels sprouts
- 4 fluid ounces (110ml) water
- 2 bay leaves
- 2 to 3 pounds (900g to 1.3kg) salted silverside

Peel potatoes, if desired. Cut parsnips or carrots into 1-inch (2.5cm) pieces. In a 3-quart (3.5l) electric slow cooker place potatoes and parsnips (see photo 1, page 55). Place frozen brussels sprouts atop vegetables in slow cooker. Add water and bay leaves. Trim excess fat from silverside. Place meat atop vegetables in cooker (see photo 3, page 55). Cover the cooker. Cook on low-heat setting for 9 to 10 hours. To serve, transfer meat to a serving plate, then thinly slice meat across the grain. Discard bay leaves. Serve vegetables with beef. Makes 6 servings.

Assembling time: 20 minutes
Cooking time: 9 to 10 hours

Keep It Covered

Be sure the lid of your slow cooker is on securely during cooking. If it isn't, the food won't cook properly. That's because cooking depends on the heat that builds up in the container itself.

Whenever you lift the cover during cooking, you'll lose heat. A quick peep will cool the food 1 or 2 degrees. And, if you leave the cooker uncovered, it can lose as much as 20°F (10°C) of cooking heat in only 2 minutes.

Fast Frittatas

Quick-cooking frittatas (*free TAHT ahs*) fit perfectly into jiffy meal plans. These open omelettes require few ingredients and little mixing. Unlike the traditional Italian frittatas, our one-step versions eliminate the grill. Simply add a lid to the frying pan and the frittata finishes cooking.

Even serving frittatas is simple. Take your frying pan right to the table!

Broccoli Frittata

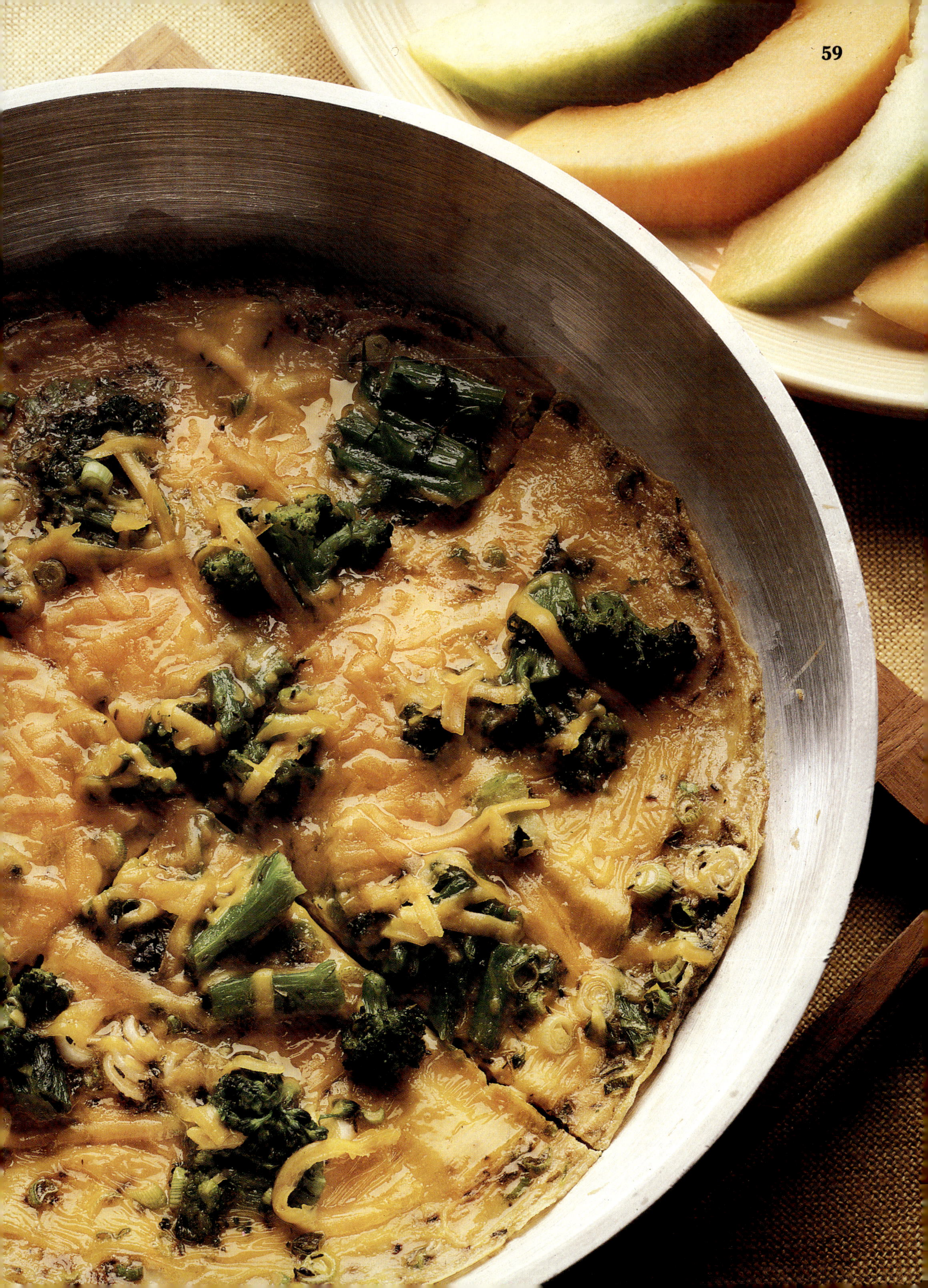

Broccoli Frittata

Buy grated cheese to save time and effort.

- 5 ounces (150g) frozen cut broccoli
- 6 eggs
- 2 spring onions, sliced
- 2 fluid ounces (55ml) simple cream *or* milk
- ½ teaspoon dried savory *or* marjoram, crushed
- ¼ teaspoon garlic salt
- Dash pepper
- 1 tablespoon cooking oil
- 2 ounces (50g) grated cheddar *or* Swiss cheese

Thaw broccoli in a colander (see photo 3, page 20). Cut up large broccoli pieces, then set aside. In a mixing bowl lightly beat eggs (see photo 1). Stir in onion, cream or milk, savory or marjoram, garlic salt, and pepper.

In a 10-inch (25.5cm) frying pan heat oil over medium-low heat until a drop of water sizzles. Add the thawed broccoli to the frying pan, then spread evenly. Pour egg mixture into frying pan over broccoli (see photo 2). Cook over medium-low heat about 10 minutes. As eggs set, run a spatula around the edge of the frying pan, lifting egg mixture to allow uncooked portion to flow underneath (see photo 3). Continue cooking and lifting edge until mixture is almost set (surface will be moist). Remove from heat.

Sprinkle cheese over top of the egg mixture. Cover frying pan; let stand 3 to 4 minutes or just until cheese is melted and top is set (see photo 4). Cut into wedges. Serve immediately. Makes 4 servings.

Assembling time: 10 minutes
Cooking time: 10 minutes
Standing time: 3 to 4 minutes

1 In a medium mixing bowl, lightly beat the eggs with a wire whisk or fork to mix the yolks and whites together, as shown. Eggs should not be frothy.

2 Spread the thawed broccoli evenly in the frying pan with the heated oil. Carefully pour the seasoned egg-cream mixture over broccoli.

3 Use medium-low heat to cook the frittata. Don't let the frying pan become too hot or the egg mixture will overcook and become tough. Run a wide spatula around the edge of the frying pan as the eggs set, lifting eggs to allow the uncooked portion to flow underneath.

4 Remove the frying pan from the heat when the eggs are almost set but still slightly shiny on their top surface. Sprinkle cheese evenly over the eggs. Cover frying pan and let frittata stand 3 to 4 minutes. The standing time allows the cheese to melt and the frittata top to finish cooking.

Chicken-Mushroom Frittata

6 eggs
2 fluid ounces (55ml) milk
1 teaspoon dried parsley
¼ teaspoon salt
¼ teaspoon dried thyme *or* tarragon, crushed
Dash pepper
5 ounces (150g) cooked chicken chunks
3 spring onions, sliced
2 ounces (50g) tinned mushrooms, drained and chopped
1 tablespoon cooking oil

In a mixing bowl lightly beat eggs (see photo 1, page 60). Stir in milk, parsley, salt, thyme or tarragon, and pepper. Stir in chicken, spring onion, and mushrooms.

In a 10-inch (25.5cm) frying pan heat oil over medium-low heat until a drop of water sizzles. Pour egg mixture into frying pan (see photo 2, page 60). Cook over medium-low heat about 10 minutes. As eggs set, run a spatula around the edge of the frying pan lifting egg mixture to allow uncooked portion to flow underneath (see photo 3, page 61). Continue cooking and lifting edge until mixture is almost set (surface will be moist).

Cover frying pan and remove from heat; let stand for 3 to 4 minutes or just until top is set (see photo 4, page 61). Cut into wedges. Serve immediately. Makes 4 servings.

Assembling time: 10 minutes
Cooking time: 10 minutes
Standing time: 3 to 4 minutes

Prawn Frittata

The prawn and colourful broccoli florets make this egg dish perfect for a special brunch.

1 small onion, chopped
2 tablespoons olive oil *or* cooking oil
4 ounces (110g) broccoli florets
4½ ounces (125g) tinned prawns,
6 eggs
2 fluid ounces (55ml) milk
2 teaspoons soy sauce
Dash pepper

In a medium saucepan cook onion in *1 tablespoon* of hot oil until onion is tender but not brown. Add broccoli, then reduce heat. Cook, covered, for 5 minutes. Rinse and drain prawns. Add prawns to broccoli and onion in saucepan.

In a mixing bowl lightly beat eggs (see photo 1, page 60). Stir in milk, soy sauce, and pepper. Stir in the prawn mixture.

In a 10-inch (25.5cm) frying pan heat remaining 1 tablespoon oil over medium-low heat until a drop of water sizzles. Pour egg mixture into frying pan (see photo 2, page 60). Cook over medium-low heat about 10 minutes. As eggs set, run a spatula around the edge of the frying pan, lifting egg mixture to allow uncooked portion to flow underneath (see photo 3, page 61). Continue cooking and lifting edge until mixture is almost set (surface will be moist).

Cover frying pan and remove from heat; let stand 3 to 4 minutes or just until top is set (see photo 4, page 61). Cut into wedges. Serve immediately. Makes 4 servings.

Assembling time: 10 minutes
Cooking time: 18 minutes
Standing time: 3 to 4 minutes

Easy Farmer's Breakfast

- 3 tablespoons cooking oil
- 12 ounces (350g) frozen potato chunks
- 1 small onion, chopped
- 1 small green pepper, chopped
- 6 eggs
- 4 ounces (110g) diced ham
- 2 fluid ounces (55ml) milk
- 1 tablespoon snipped chives
- ¼ teaspoon salt
- Few dashes bottled hot pepper sauce
- Dash pepper

In a 10-inch (25.5cm) frying pan heat oil over medium heat. Add frozen potatoes to frying pan according to package directions. Add onion and green pepper. Cook, covered, for 8 to 10 minutes, stirring once or twice.

Meanwhile, in a mixing bowl lightly beat eggs (see photo 1, page 60). Stir in ham, milk, chives, salt, hot pepper sauce, and pepper. Pour the egg mixture into frying pan over potato mixture (see photo 2, page 60). Cook over medium-low heat about 10 minutes. As eggs set, run a spatula around the edge of the frying pan lifting egg mixture to allow uncooked portion to flow underneath (see photo 3, page 61). Continue cooking and lifting edge until mixture is almost set (surface will be moist).

Cover frying pan and remove from heat; let stand 3 to 4 minutes or just until top is set (see photo 4, page 61). Cut into wedges. Serve immediately. Makes 4 servings.

Assembling time: 10 minutes
Cooking time: 20 minutes
Standing time: 3 to 4 minutes

Pepperoni Frittata

Pepperoni adds flavour in two places—in the frittata itself and in the sauce served over the frittata.

- 3 ounces (85g) cream cheese
- 4 ounces (110g) pepperoni, sliced
- 8 fluid ounces (220ml) prepared pizza sauce
- 3 ounces (75g) tinned sliced mushrooms, drained
- 2 fluid ounces (55ml) milk
- 6 eggs
- ¼ teaspoon salt
- Dash pepper
- 1 ounce (25g) butter *or* margarine

Cut cheese into cubes, then set aside. If pepperoni slices are large, cut them into quarters. In a saucepan combine pizza sauce, mushrooms, and *half* of the pepperoni. Cook over low heat, uncovered, for 10 to 15 minutes.

Meanwhile, in a blender or food processor bowl combine the cheese cubes and milk. Cover and blend or process until smooth. Add eggs, salt, and pepper. Cover and blend or process 10 seconds. Stir in remaining pepperoni.

In a 10-inch (25.5cm) frying pan heat butter or margarine over medium-low heat. Pour egg mixture into frying pan (see photo 2, page 60). Cook over medium-low heat about 10 minutes. As eggs set, run a spatula around the edge of the frying pan, lifting egg mixture to allow uncooked portion to flow underneath (see photo 3, page 61). Continue cooking and lifting edge until almost set (surface will be moist).

Cover frying pan and remove from heat; let stand 3 to 4 minutes or just until the top is set (see photo 4, page 61). Cut into wedges. Spoon some pizza sauce mixture over top, then pass remaining sauce separately. Serve immediately. Makes 4 servings.

Assembling time: 20 minutes
Cooking time: 10 minutes
Standing time: 3 to 4 minutes

Quick-Cooked Frozen Fish

Here's some great news! Don't waste your time waiting for fish to thaw. Instead, poach fish that's still frozen. Then, serve the fish with an easy-to-make sauce or feature it in a main-dish salad.

Save more time—and money, too—by stocking your freezer with a favourite variety of fish. A delicious meal is only a few minutes away!

65

Orange-Poached Fish

Orange-Poached Fish

7 ounces (200g) long grain rice
16 ounces (450g) frozen fish fillets
4 medium carrots
1 stalk celery
8 fluid ounces (220ml) orange juice
¼ teaspoon salt
¼ teaspoon dried basil, crushed
Dash pepper
1 tablespoon cornflour
1 tablespoon cold water
Orange slices
Cucumber slices

Prepare rice according to packet directions. Meanwhile, place frozen block of fish in an ungreased 10-inch (25.5cm) frying pan. Slice carrots ¼ inch (.5cm) thick and celery ½ inch (1cm) thick (see photo 1). Add carrots and celery to the frying pan. Stir together orange juice, salt, basil, and pepper, then add to the fish. Bring mixture to the boil. Reduce heat to simmering (see photo 2). Cook, covered, 15 to 20 minutes or until fish tests done (see photo 3).

Spread rice on a warm serving dish. Divide fish into four portions. Remove fish and vegetables from the frying pan with a slotted spoon and arrange over rice on the serving dish. Reserve cooking liquid. Cover dish to keep food warm.

To make sauce, measure cooking liquid (if necessary, add water to measure 8 fluid ounces (220 ml)). Strain liquid, if desired, then pour into the frying pan. Stir together cornflour and water, then add to liquid in the frying pan. Cook and stir until thickened and bubbly, then cook and stir 2 minutes more. Pour sauce over fish and vegetables. Garnish with orange- and cucumber-slice twists (see photo 4). Serve immediately. Makes 4 servings.

Assembling time: 15 minutes
Cooking time: 20 to 25 minutes

1 Slicing on the diagonal gives fresh vegetables extra eye-appeal. And it's so easy. Using a sharp knife, make the first cut on a diagonal. Follow through with the same angle for remaining cuts, slicing vegetables into pieces of even thickness.

2 Bring the orange juice mixture to the boil. Then, reduce heat to simmering. The mixture is simmering when a few bubbles form slowly and burst before they reach the surface. Cover frying pan.

3 When the fish is done, it becomes opaque, white, and tender. Test to see if the fish is done by inserting fork prongs into the fish at a 45-degree angle. Twist the fork gently. The fish is done if it flakes, as shown. If the fish resists flaking and still has a translucent quality, it's not done. If it's dry and mealy, the fish has cooked too long.

4 Decorate the serving dish with a colourful garnish. Orange and cucumber slices are a quick trim. First, make a cut just to the centre of an orange slice. Then, twist the cut ends of the orange in opposite directions. Use the same technique with cucumber (or lemon) slices. For an even more colourful look, twist an orange and a cucumber slice together.

Fish with Cream Sauce

Enhance your favourite fish with this simple, delicate sauce—it's flavoured with bay leaves.

16	ounces (450g) frozen fish fillets
12	fluid ounces (330ml) water
2	tablespoons lemon juice
4	bay leaves
1	teaspoon instant chicken bouillon granules
3	fluid ounces (80ml) single cream
4	teaspoons cornflour
2	tablespoons snipped parsley
	Lemon slices

Place frozen fish in an ungreased 10-inch (25.5cm) frying pan. Add water, lemon juice, bay leaves, and bouillon granules. Bring mixture to the boil. Reduce heat to simmering (see photo 2, page 67). Cook, covered, 15 to 20 minutes or until fish tests done (see photo 3, page 67). Remove fish from frying pan with a slotted spoon and place on a warm dish. Reserve cooking liquid. Cover dish to keep fish warm.

To make sauce, strain 8 fluid ounces (220ml) cooking liquid. Discard remaining liquid and bay leaves. Pour strained liquid into the frying pan. Shake cream and cornflour together (see photo 2, page 43). Stir mixture into the liquid in the frying pan. Cook and stir until thickened and bubbly, then cook and stir 2 minutes more. Stir in parsley. Pour sauce over the fish. Garnish with lemon-slice twists (see photo 4, page 67). Makes 4 servings.

Assembling time: 15 minutes
Cooking time: 20 to 25 minutes

Italian-Style Fish

2	spring onions, sliced
1	tablespoon cooking oil
8	ounces (225g) tinned sieved tomatoes
½	teaspoon caster sugar
½	teaspoon dried thyme, crushed
⅛	teaspoon garlic powder
1	pound (450g) individually frozen fish fillets
12	fluid ounces (330ml) water
½	teaspoon dried basil, crushed
1	ounce (25g) grated Parmesan cheese

In a small saucepan cook spring onion in hot oil until tender but not brown. Stir in sieved tomatoes, sugar, thyme, and garlic powder. Bring mixture to the boil. Reduce heat, then simmer sauce, uncovered, about 10 minutes.

Meanwhile, place frozen fish in an ungreased 10-inch (25.5cm) frying pan. Add water and basil. Bring mixture to the boil. Reduce heat to simmering (see photo 2, page 67). Cook, covered, about 4 minutes for ¼-inch (.5cm) fillets (about 8 minutes for ½-inch [1cm] fillets) or until fish tests done (see photo 3, page 67). Transfer fish to a warm serving dish. Pour hot sauce over fillets. Sprinkle Parmesan cheese over fillets. Serve immediately. Serves 4.

Assembling time: 10 minutes
Cooking time: 10 minutes

Buying Frozen Fish

Learn to be a smart fish shopper, and you'll never be disappointed with your purchases. Select packets of frozen fish that have their wrapping intact. Also, choose frost-free packets for the best possible product.

California Fish Salad

16 ounces (450g) frozen fish fillets
24 fluid ounces (680ml) water
1 small onion
1 stalk celery
1 small iceberg lettuce, washed and torn
6 ounces (175g) cherry tomatoes, halved
2 ounces (55ml) grated Edam cheese
4 fluid ounces (110ml) bottled creamy coleslaw salad dressing

Place frozen fish in an ungreased 10-inch (25.5cm) frying pan. Add water to the frying pan. Bring water to the boil. Reduce heat to simmering (see photo 2, page 67). Cook, covered, 15 to 20 minutes or until fish tests done (see photo 3, page 67).

Lift fish to a plate with a slotted spoon or spatula. Break fish into 1-inch (2.5cm) chunks. Cover and place in the freezer, if desired, to chill while preparing rest of salad.

Cut onion into thin slices and separate into rings. Slice celery ¼ inch (.5cm) thick (see photo 1, page 66). Place lettuce in a large salad bowl. Add onion rings, celery, and tomatoes. Sprinkle with cheese. Arrange fish chunks on top. Drizzle coleslaw salad dressing over assembled salad. Lightly toss ingredients together. Makes 4 servings.

Assembling time: 20 minutes
Cooking time: 15 to 20 minutes

Wine-Sauced Fish Steaks

Look no further for a delicious seafood dish that serves just two!

2 frozen halibut *or* salmon steaks, cut ½ to ¾ inch (1 to 2cm) thick (about 10 ounces [275g] total)
12 fluid ounces (330ml) water
1 teaspoon instant chicken bouillon granules
½ teaspoon dried rosemary, crushed
1 ounce (25g) butter *or* margarine
1 tablespoon cornflour
2 fluid ounces (55ml) dry white wine
10 ounces (275g) cooked rice
Parsley sprigs (optional)
Lemon slices (optional)

Place frozen fish in an ungreased 10-inch (25.5cm) frying pan. Stir together water, bouillon granules, and rosemary, then add to the fish in frying pan. Bring mixture to the boil. Reduce heat to simmering (see photo 2, page 67). Cook, covered, 8 to 10 minutes or until fish tests done (see photo 3, page 67).

Remove fish from the frying pan, reserving cooking liquid. Keep fish warm. To make sauce, strain cooking liquid into a glass measure and reserve 6 fluid ounces (165ml) liquid.

In the same frying pan melt butter or margarine. Stir in cornflour, then stir in 6 fluid ounces (165ml) reserved cooking liquid. Cook and stir until mixture is thickened and bubbly. Stir in wine, then cook and stir sauce 2 minutes more.

To serve, spread rice on a warm serving dish. Arrange fish over rice. Spoon sauce over fish. Garnish with parsley and lemon-slice twists, if desired (see photo 4, page 67). Serve immediately. Makes 2 servings.

Assembling time: 15 minutes
Cooking time: 13 to 15 minutes

Versatile Meat Make-Aheads

Saving time by planning ahead is often easier said than done. With these recipes, however, it *is* easy to do. Get much of the work out of the way when you've got some spare time. How?

Make a basic minced meat mixture and freeze it in small portions. Then, when there's little time in your schedule for cooking, build on the base by adding ingredients to make a variety of main dishes.

Hearty Open Sandwiches

Minced Meat Freezer Base

Use half beef and half pork to make a tasty combination of meat flavours.

- 3 slices bread
- 3 eggs
- 5 ounces (150g) chopped celery
- 8 ounces (225g) chopped onion
- 5 ounces (150g) shredded carrot
- 1 teaspoon salt
- 3 pounds (1kg350g) minced beef *or* minced pork

Cut bread slices into quarters, then place in a blender or a food processor bowl. Cover and blend or process until crumbs are fine and even (see photo 1).

In a large bowl beat eggs. Stir in crumbs, celery, onion, carrot, and salt. Add minced beef or pork and mix well.

In a large frying pan cook meat mixture, half at a time, over medium-high heat until meat is brown. Stir to break up large pieces of meat. Drain off fat. Cool quickly (see photo 2).

Spoon about *15 ounces (425g)* of the meat mixture into *each* of five freezer bags or wraps. Seal, label, and freeze. Makes five 15-ounce (425g) portions.

Assembling time: 30 minutes
Cooking time: 30 minutes

1 Place bread in a blender or a food processor bowl. Cover and blend or process until the texture of crumbs is fine and even. Pour crumbs onto a scale and measure 9 ounces (250g).

2 Line a shallow tin with kitchen paper. Using a slotted spoon, transfer the cooked meat mixture to the paper-lined tin. Spread meat out so that it cools quickly. The kitchen paper absorbs the additional fat that drains off.

Hearty Open Sandwiches

1 15-ounce (425g) portion Minced Meat Freezer Base (see recipe opposite)
2 fluid ounces (55ml) water
9 ounces (250g) tinned whole kernel sweet corn, drained
6 fluid ounces (165ml) bottled barbecue sauce
4 wedges corn bread, split, *or* 4 baps, split and toasted
Natural yogurt (optional)

Thaw Minced Meat Freezer Base in a medium saucepan with water (see photo 3). Cover and cook over medium-low heat about 15 minutes; break up meat with a fork (see photo 4). Cover and cook 5 minutes more.

Stir corn and barbecue sauce into meat mixture. Cook and stir until mixture is heated through. Spoon meat mixture over corn bread (see photo 5). Or, spoon meat into toasted baps. Pass yogurt to spoon on top, if desired. Makes 4 servings.

Assembling time: 10 minutes
Cooking time: 25 minutes

4 Use a fork to break apart the frozen mixture as it begins to thaw. Breaking it up speeds the thawing time. Be sure to use medium-low heat to prevent scorching the mixture during heating.

5 To serve, split wedges of corn bread in half and spoon the hot meat-corn mixture over both halves. Or, leave the corn bread wedge or square in one piece and spoon the mixture over the top.

3 To use a portion without waiting hours for it to thaw in the refrigerator, place the frozen block of meat in a saucepan. Then, add the measured amount of water.

Meaty Cream Cheese Stroganoff

If the shop doesn't have cream cheese with chives, substitute plain cream cheese. Then, stir in 2 tablespoons of snipped chives.

- 1 15-ounce (425g) portion Minced Meat Freezer Base (see recipe, page 72)
- 2 fluid ounces (55ml) water
- 2½ ounces (60g) tinned sliced mushrooms, drained
- 6 ounces (175g) cream cheese with chives
- 4 fluid ounces (110ml) milk
- Hot cooked noodles
- Paprika

Thaw Minced Meat Freezer Base in a medium saucepan with water (see photo 3, page 73). Cover and cook over medium-low heat about 15 minutes; break up meat with a fork (see photo 4, page 73). Cover; cook 5 minutes more.

Stir in mushrooms. Cut cream cheese into cubes, then stir cheese and milk into meat mixture. Cook and stir over low heat until smooth and heated through. Serve over noodles. Sprinkle with paprika. Makes 4 servings.

Assembling time: 5 minutes
Cooking time: 25 to 30 minutes

Frying Pan Stuffed Peppers

You save valuable time by steaming the green peppers and thawing the meat in the same frying pan.

- 1 15-ounce (425g) portion Minced Meat Freezer Base (see recipe, page 72)
- 4 fluid ounces (110ml) water
- 2 green peppers
- 16 ounces (450g) tinned tomatoes
- 4 ounces (110g) quick-cooking rice
- 1 teaspoon Worcestershire sauce
- 4 ounces (110g) processed cheese

Place Minced Meat Freezer Base in a 10-inch (25.5cm) frying pan with water (see photo 3, page 73). Cut green peppers in half lengthwise, then discard seeds and membrane. Arrange pepper halves, cut sides down, around edges of the frying pan. Cover and cook over medium-low heat about 15 minutes; break up meat with a fork (see photo 4, page 73). Remove green peppers, then drain. Cover and keep warm. Drain off cooking liquid in frying pan.

Cut up tomatoes (see photo 2, page 20). Add *undrained* tomatoes, *uncooked* rice, and Worcestershire sauce to meat mixture in the frying pan. Bring to the boil. Reduce heat, then simmer, covered, about 5 minutes or until rice is tender.

Put cheese on top of meat mixture. Heat and stir until cheese is melted. To serve, place green pepper halves upright on dinner plates, then spoon in meat mixture. Makes 4 servings.

Assembling time: 10 minutes
Cooking time: 25 minutes

Scone-Topped Frying Pan Supper

Keep ingredients for this dish on hand. Then, when you're in a pinch, fix this meal in about 40 minutes.

- 1 15-ounce (425g) portion Minced Meat Freezer Base (see recipe, page 72)
- 2 fluid ounces (55ml) water
- 11 fluid ounces (325ml) tinned condensed cream of onion soup
- 4 fluid ounces (110ml) milk
- 16 ounces (450g) tinned cut green beans, drained
- 8 ounces (225g) tinned whole water chestnuts, drained and sliced
- 1 teaspoon dried basil, crushed
- ¼ teaspoon pepper
- 1 packet (6) refrigerated scones

Thaw Minced Meat Freezer Base in a 10-inch (25.5cm) oven-proof frying pan with water (see photo 3, page 73). Cover and cook over medium-low heat about 15 minutes; break up meat with a fork (see photo 4, page 73). Cover and cook the mixture 5 minutes more.

Stir soup and milk into meat mixture. Stir in beans, water chestnuts, basil, and pepper, then heat and stir until bubbly.

Separate each scone into two thinner scones. Arrange scones around edge of *bubbling* meat mixture in the frying pan, overlapping to fit. Bake in a 450°F (230°C) gas mark 8 oven for 10 to 12 minutes or until scones are golden. Makes 4 servings.

Assembling time: 5 minutes
Cooking time: 35 to 37 minutes

Chilli-Bean Dish

- 1 15-ounce (425g) portion Minced Meat Freezer Base (see recipe, page 72)
- 10 ounces (275g) tinned tomatoes and green chilli peppers
- 8 ounces (225g) tinned red kidney beans, drained
- 8 ounces (225g) tinned sieved tomatoes
- 1 to 2 teaspoons chilli powder
- 4 ounces (110g) grated cheddar cheese

Thaw Minced Meat Freezer Base in a large saucepan with 2 fluid ounces (55ml) *water* (see photo 3, page 73). Cover and cook over medium-low heat about 15 minutes; break up meat with a fork (see photo 4, page 73). Cover and cook 5 minutes more. Stir tomatoes and green chilli peppers, kidney beans, sieved tomatoes, and chilli powder into meat mixture in the saucepan. Bring to the boil. Reduce heat, then simmer, uncovered, about 10 minutes or to the desired consistency. Spoon into serving bowls. Sprinkle cheese over each serving. Serve with potato crisps, if desired. Makes 4 servings.

Assembling time: 5 minutes
Cooking time: 30 minutes

Thawing the Minced Meat Freezer Base

Thawing times differ slightly depending on whether you freeze the base in a freezer container or bag. It takes about 15 minutes to thaw the block from a freezer container using a little liquid in a pan. Or, shorten the thawing time by freezing the base in a ½- to 1-inch (1 to 2.5cm) layer in a freezer bag. Thaw base in 5 to 10 minutes.

Oriental Beef

You'll get lots of crunch in this minced meat dish from the water chestnuts and chow mein noodles.

- 1 15-ounce (425g) portion Minced Meat Freezer Base (see recipe, page 72)
- 5 fluid ounces (140ml) water
- ½ teaspoon instant beef bouillon granules
- 6 ounces (175g) frozen mange tout
- 4 ounces (110g) tinned water chestnuts, sliced
- 2 tablespoons soy sauce
- 2 tablespoons dry sherry
- 1 tablespoon cornflour
- ½ teaspoon caster sugar
- ¼ teaspoon ground ginger *or* five-spice powder
- Chow mein noodles

Thaw Minced Meat Freezer Base in a medium saucepan with water and bouillon granules (see photo 3, page 73). Cover and cook the mixture over medium-low heat about 15 minutes; break up meat with a fork (see photo 4, page 73). Cover and cook 5 minutes more.

Meanwhile, run warm water over frozen mange tout to separate (see photo 3, page 20). Drain. Add mange tout to meat mixture; cover and cook 2 to 3 minutes more or until heated through. Add water chestnuts.

In a small bowl stir together soy sauce, sherry, cornflour, sugar, and ginger or five-spice powder. Stir into beef mixture. Cook and stir until thickened and bubbly, then cook and stir 2 minutes more. Serve over chow mein noodles. Makes 3 servings.

Assembling time: 5 minutes
Cooking time: 28 to 30 minutes

Dilled Meat and Potato Chowder

- 1 15-ounce (425g) portion Minced Meat Freezer Base (see recipe, page 72)
- 2 fluid ounces (55ml) water
- 12 fluid ounces (330ml) water
- 6 ounces (175g) sliced potato
- 2 teaspoons instant beef bouillon granules
- ½ teaspoon dried dill
- 8 fluid ounces (220ml) milk
- 3 tablespoons plain flour
- ⅛ teaspoon pepper

Thaw Minced Meat Freezer Base in a medium saucepan with 2 fluid ounces (55ml) water (see photo 3, page 73). Cover and cook over medium-low heat about 15 minutes; break up meat with a fork (see photo 4, page 73). Cover and cook 5 minutes more.

Drain off cooking liquid. Stir 12 fluid ounces (220ml) water, potato, bouillon granules, and dill into meat mixture. Bring mixture to the boil. Reduce heat, then simmer, covered, for 8 to 10 minutes or until potato is tender.

Meanwhile, combine milk, flour, and pepper in a screw-top jar; shake well (see photo 2, page 43). Stir into beef-potato mixture. Cook and stir until thickened and bubbly, then cook and stir 1 minute more. Makes 4 servings.

Assembling time: 5 minutes
Cooking time: 35 to 40 minutes

Sweet-Sour Beef And Vegetable Salad

While the meat simmers, fix the salad ingredients—spinach or lettuce, mushrooms, and onion. That way, everything's ready to serve at once.

- 1 15-ounce (425g) portion Minced Meat Freezer Base (see recipe, page 72)
- 2 fluid ounces (55ml) tarragon vinegar
- 2 tablespoons water
- 2 tablespoons lemon juice
- 1 tablespoon cooking oil
- 8 ounces (225g) torn fresh spinach *or* lettuce
- 3 ounces (75g) sliced fresh mushrooms
- 1 small onion, thinly sliced and separated into rings
- 2 tablespoons soft brown sugar
- 1 tablespoon cold water
- 1 teaspoon cornflour
- 11 ounces (300g) tinned mandarin oranges, drained

Thaw Minced Meat Freezer Base in a 10-inch (25.5cm) frying pan with vinegar, 2 tablespoons water, lemon juice, and cooking oil (see photo 3, page 73). Cover and cook over medium-low heat about 15 minutes; break up meat with a fork (see photo 4, page 73). Cover and cook 5 minutes more.

Meanwhile, in a salad bowl combine spinach or lettuce, mushrooms, and onion. Stir together sugar, 1 tablespoon water, and cornflour; stir into meat mixture. Cook and stir until thickened and bubbly, then cook and stir 2 minutes more.

Spoon meat mixture atop ingredients in salad bowl. Garnish with mandarin oranges. Toss mixture together. Serve immediately. Serves 4.

Assembling time: 5 minutes
Cooking time: 25 minutes

Creamed Peas and Beef

No vol-au-vent cases on hand? This creamy mixture also tastes fantastic over toast points or biscuits.

- 4 frozen vol-au-vent cases
- 1 15-ounce (425g) portion Minced Meat Freezer Base (see recipe, page 72)
- 2 fluid ounces (55ml) water
- 10 ounces frozen peas
- ½ pint (275ml) tinned condensed cream of mushroom soup
- ¼ pint (150ml) milk
- 3 ounces (75g) tinned sliced mushrooms, drained
- 1 tablespoon dry sherry

Prepare vol-au-vent cases according to packet directions. Meanwhile, thaw Minced Meat Freezer Base in a 3¼-pint (1.75l) saucepan with water (see photo 3, page 73). Cover and cook over medium-low heat about 15 minutes; break up meat with a fork (see photo 4, page 73). Cover and cook 5 minutes more.

Stir in frozen peas, soup, and milk. Cover and cook 8 to 10 minutes more or until peas are tender, stirring twice.

Stir mushrooms and sherry into mixture. Heat through. Spoon creamed mixture into vol-au-vent cases. Makes 4 servings.

Assembling time: 5 minutes
Cooking time: 30 to 35 minutes

Double-Duty Entrées

Cook these recipes two batches at a time and you've prepared two meals at once. Serve half now— freeze the other half for dinner number two. The convenience becomes apparent when you discover the minimal preparation and clearing up needed for the second meal. Give our recipes in this section a try. Then use this shortcut trick on some of your own main-dish favourites.

Stew with Potato Topper

Potato Topper

2	pounds (900g) stewing beef *or* boneless pork, cut into 1-inch (2.5cm) cubes
2	tablespoons cooking oil
16	fluid ounces (440ml) apple juice
8	fluid ounces (220ml) water
1½	teaspoons salt
½	teaspoon dried thyme, crushed
¼	teaspoon pepper
1	bay leaf
2	medium onions, cut into wedges
4	fluid ounces (110ml) water
2	tablespoons quick-cooking tapioca
2	teaspoons dried parsley
24	ounces (700g) frozen crinkle-cut carrots
9	ounces (250g) frozen cut green beans
	Packet instant mashed potatoes (enough for 4 servings)
	Paprika (optional)

In a large covered casserole or large saucepan cook *half* of the meat in hot oil until brown. Remove meat with a slotted spoon; set aside. Repeat with remaining meat. Drain off fat. Return all meat to pan.

Stir in apple juice, 8 fluid ounces (220ml) water, salt, thyme, pepper, and bay leaf. Add onions to meat mixture. Bring mixture to the boil. Reduce heat, then simmer, covered, about 1½ hours for beef (or about 45 minutes for pork) or until meat is nearly tender.

Meanwhile, stir together 4 fluid ounces (110ml) water and tapioca; let stand 5 minutes. Stir tapioca mixture and parsley into stew, then add carrots and beans. Return to the boil, stirring occasionally. Reduce heat, then simmer, covered, about 5 minutes more or just until vegetables are tender, stirring occasionally. Discard bay leaf. Transfer *half* of the stew to a pan or bowl (see photo 1). Cool quickly (see photo 2). Transfer the cooled stew to a freezer container; seal, label, and freeze.

Prepare mashed potatoes according to packet directions. Ladle remaining hot stew into individual bowls. Spoon potatoes atop stew in large dollops. Sprinkle with paprika, if desired. Makes two portions, 4 servings each.

Assembling time: 30 minutes
Cooking time (beef): 1 hour 35 minutes (pork): 50 minutes

To serve the frozen portion: Place freezer container in warm water to loosen stew (see photo 3). Transfer stew to a medium saucepan. Add 2 fluid ounces (55ml) *water* to saucepan (see photo 3, page 73). Cook, covered, over medium-low heat 30 to 35 minutes or until thawed, breaking apart with a fork occasionally (see photo 4, page 73). Heat through. Meanwhile, prepare 4-serving packet instant *mashed potatoes* according to packet directions. Serve as above.

Final preparation time: 35 to 40 minutes

1 Using a long-handled cup or a ladle, transfer *half* of the stew to a metal pan or bowl. This portion of stew is cooled and frozen for another meal. Keep remaining stew hot to serve at once.

2 Quickly cool hot stew by placing pan in a larger dish or bowl filled with ice cubes and cold water. Quick cooling is important for food safety. It stops the cooking as well as slows the growth of bacteria in the food. After cooling, immediately transfer mixture to a freezer container.

3 To loosen the frozen mixture from the container, place the covered freezer container in a bowl of warm water. Then, transfer the frozen mixture to a cooking pan.

Penne with Italian Sauce

Serve some crusty bread or rolls with this main dish.

- 12 ounces (350g) minced beef
- 12 ounces (350g) spicy sausage meat
- 1 onion, chopped
- 1 clove garlic, minced
- 32 ounces (900g) tinned tomatoes
- 8 ounces (225g) tinned sieved tomatoes
- 6 ounces (175g) tomato puree
- 2 teaspoons dried basil, crushed
- 3½ ounces (85g) sliced pepperoni
- 12 ounces (350g) penne
- Grated Parmesan cheese

In a saucepan cook beef, sausage, onion, and garlic until meat is brown. Drain off fat. Cut up tomatoes (see photo 2, page 20). Stir *undrained* tomatoes, sieved tomatoes, tomato puree, and basil into meat mixture. Simmer, covered, for 30 minutes. Halve pepperoni slices; stir into meat. Cook 15 minutes more. Skim off fat.

Meanwhile, cook penne according to packet directions until just tender (do not overcook); drain. Place *half* of the penne in a metal tin or bowl. Pour *half* of the meat mixture (about 4 cups) over penne in tin (see photo 1, page 81). Stir together. Cool quickly (see photo 2, page 81). Transfer to a freezer container; seal, label, and freeze. Add remaining penne to remaining meat mixture in saucepan; toss to coat. Pass Parmesan cheese. Makes two portions, 4 servings each.

Total preparation time: 70 minutes

To serve the frozen portion: Place freezer container in warm water to loosen mixture (see photo 3, page 81). Transfer the mixture to a large saucepan. Add 4 fluid ounces (110ml) *water* to saucepan (see photo 3, page 73). Cook, covered, over medium-low heat for 30 to 35 minutes or until thawed, breaking apart with a fork occasionally (see photo 4, page 73). Heat through. Pass grated *Parmesan cheese*.

Final preparation time: 35 to 40 minutes

Saucy Orange Beef

- 1½ pounds (700g) boneless beef, cut into thin bite-size strips
- 2 tablespoons cooking oil
- 14 fluid ounces (385ml) orange juice
- 3 fluid ounces (80ml) dry sherry
- 2 fluid ounces (55ml) soy sauce
- 2 cloves garlic, minced
- ½ teaspoon ground ginger
- 3 tablespoons cornflour
- 8 ounces (225g) tinned whole water chestnuts, drained and sliced
- 16 ounces (450g) frozen mixed green beans, broccoli, onions, and mushrooms
- **Hot cooked rice**

In a large frying pan brown meat, half at a time, in hot oil. Return all meat to the frying pan. Stir in orange juice, sherry, soy sauce, garlic, and ginger. Simmer, covered, for 20 minutes. Combine cornflour and 3 fluid ounces (80ml) *cold water*. Stir into mixture in frying pan. Cook and stir until thickened and bubbly, then cook and stir 2 minutes more. Remove from heat. Stir in water chestnuts. Transfer *half* of the mixture to a pan or bowl (see photo 1, page 81). Cool quickly (see photo 2, page 81). Transfer to a freezer container; seal, label, and freeze. Stir the 16 ounces (450g) vegetables into remaining mixture. Simmer, covered, about 8 minutes or until vegetables are tender. Serve over rice. Makes two portions, 4 servings each.

Total preparation time: 55 minutes

To serve the frozen portion: Place freezer container in warm water to loosen mixture (see photo 3, page 81). Transfer to a saucepan. Add 2 fluid ounces (55ml) *water* (see photo 3, page 73). Cook, covered, over medium-low heat 20 to 25 minutes or until thawed, breaking apart with a fork (see photo 4, page 73). Stir in 16 ounces (450g) frozen mixed *green beans, broccoli, onions, and mushrooms*. Simmer, covered, about 8 minutes or until vegetables are tender. Serve over hot cooked *rice*.

Final preparation time: 30 to 35 minutes

Prawns in Cheddar Sauce

6	frozen vol-au-vent cases
16	ounces (450g) frozen peas
8	ounces (225g) frozen cooked prawns
4	spring onions, chopped
4	ounces (110g) butter *or* margarine
3½	ounces (85g) plain flour
½	teaspoon paprika
1¼	pints (720ml) milk
4	fluid ounces (110ml) dry white wine
8	ounces (225g) grated cheddar cheese

Bake vol-au-vent cases according to packet directions. Meanwhile, run warm water over frozen peas. Run warm water over prawns to thaw (see photo 3, page 20). Drain peas and prawns well; set aside. In a saucepan cook onion in butter or margarine until tender. Stir in flour, paprika, and ¼ teaspoon *pepper*. Stir in milk. Cook and stir until thickened and bubbly, then cook and stir 1 minute more. Stir in wine. Add peas and cheddar cheese; heat and stir until cheese melts.

Transfer *half* of the mixture to a pan or bowl (see photo 1, page 81). Cool quickly (see photo 2, page 81). Transfer to a freezer container; seal, label, and freeze. Stir prawns into remaining mixture; heat through. Serve at once in vol-au-vent cases. Makes two portions, 6 servings each.

Total preparation time: 35 minutes

To serve the frozen portion: Place freezer container in warm water to loosen mixture (see photo 3, page 81). Transfer mixture to a saucepan. Cook, covered, over medium heat 5 minutes. Reduce heat to medium-low and cook about 20 minutes; stir frequently. Meanwhile, bake 6 frozen *vol-au-vent cases* according to packet directions. Run warm water over 8 ounces (225g) *frozen cooked prawns* in a colander; drain well. Add prawns to mixture in saucepan; cook 10 minutes or until hot. Serve at once in vol-au-vent cases as above.

Final preparation time: 35 minutes

Cranberry-Peach Ham

16	ounces (450g) frozen crinkle-cut carrots
12	fluid ounces (330ml) water
10	fluid ounces (275ml) cranberry sauce
4	fluid ounces (110ml) chilli sauce
1½	pounds (700g) ham, cooked, cut into ½-inch (1cm) cubes
3	fluid ounces (80ml) cold water
3	tablespoons cornflour
16	ounces (450g) tinned peach slices, drained
	Hot cooked rice

In a frying pan combine frozen carrots, 12 fluid ounces (330ml) water, cranberry sauce, and chilli sauce. Bring to the boil. Reduce heat, then simmer, covered, for 10 minutes. Stir in ham.

Combine 3 fluid ounces (80ml) water and cornflour. Stir into mixture in frying pan. Cook and stir until thickened and bubbly, then cook and stir 2 minutes more. Transfer *half* of the mixture to a pan or bowl (see photo 1, page 81). Cool quickly (see photo 2, page 81). Transfer to a freezer container; seal, label, and freeze. Cut peach slices in half, if desired. Stir peaches into remaining ham mixture; heat through. Serve over rice. Makes two portions, 4 servings each.

Total preparation time: 35 minutes

To serve the frozen portion: Place freezer container in warm water to loosen mixture (see photo 3, page 81). Transfer mixture to a medium saucepan. Add 2 fluid ounces (55ml) *water* to saucepan (see photo 3, page 73). Cook, covered, over medium-low heat for 30 to 35 minutes or until thawed, breaking apart with a fork occasionally (see photo 4, page 73). Drain 16 ounces (450g) tinned *peach slices;* cut slices in half, if desired. Stir peaches into meat mixture; heat through. Serve over hot cooked *rice*.

Final preparation time: 35 to 40 minutes

Kababs on the Grill

The smaller the pieces of food, the faster they cook. That's why kababs are such a great way to save time. Also, these kababs are practically a whole meal-on-a-skewer. While the kababs grill, cook some noodles, toss together a salad, and dinner is ready.

Teriyaki Chicken Kababs

Teriyaki Chicken Kababs

1¼ pounds (560g) boneless, skinned chicken breasts
3 fluid ounces (80ml) teriyaki sauce
2 fluid ounces (55ml) cooking oil
2 fluid ounces (55ml) dry white wine
1 tablespoon lemon juice
¼ teaspoon onion powder *or* dried onion flakes
2 stalks celery*
1 papaya

Cut chicken into strips (see photo 1). For marinade, in a bowl stir together teriyaki sauce, oil, wine, lemon juice, and onion powder. Add chicken strips, then stir to coat well. Cover and marinate 20 minutes at room temperature or 8 to 24 hours in the refrigerator; stir occasionally.

Preheat the grill. Meanwhile, cut celery into 1-inch (2.5cm) pieces. Seed and peel papaya (see photo 2). Cut into 1-inch (2.5cm) pieces. Drain chicken strips and reserve marinade. For the kababs, thread chicken strips alternately with celery and papaya onto eight 8- or 9-inch (20 or 23cm) skewers (see photo 3).

Place kababs on the *unheated* rack of a grill pan. Place kababs 3 to 4 inches (7.5 to 10cm) from the heat (see photo 4). Grill for 5 minutes. Brush kababs with reserved marinade (see photo 5). Turn kababs and brush again with marinade. Grill 5 to 6 minutes more or until chicken is done. Brush again with reserved marinade. Makes 4 servings.

*Note: If desired, cut 1 large *red or green pepper* into 1-inch (2.5cm) squares and substitute for all or part of the celery pieces.

Assembling time: 30 minutes
Marinating time: 20 minutes to 24 hours
Cooking time: 10 to 11 minutes

1 Place boned chicken breasts on a cutting surface. Using a sharp knife, cut chicken into ¾- to 1-inch (2 to 2.5cm) strips, making the strips as long as possible. The longer the strips, the easier they will be to thread onto the skewers.

2 Select a ripe, yet firm papaya. First, cut the papaya in half lengthwise. Scoop out the black seeds that fill centre cavity. Cut off the thin skin from each half using a small paring knife. Finally, cut the fruit into 1-inch (2.5cm) pieces.

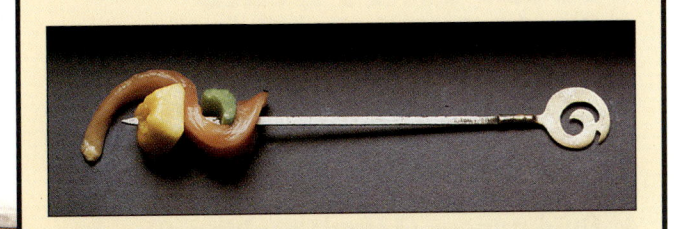

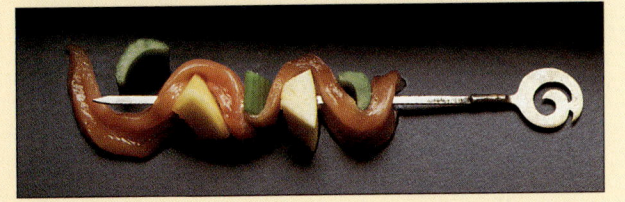

3 To thread kababs, skewer one end of a chicken strip. Next, add a celery, papaya, or pepper piece. Then, thread another portion of chicken strip onto skewer and another fruit or vegetable piece, as shown (top). If strip is long enough, continue with chicken and fruit or vegetable pieces. Repeat threading of chicken and fruit and vegetable pieces on the same skewer, as shown (bottom). Repeat for rest of skewers.

4 Place kababs on the unheated rack of a grill pan. Place pan under grill so that the top surface of the kababs is 3 to 4 inches (7.5 to 10cm) from the heat source. Use a ruler to measure the distance. If you place kababs closer than 3 inches (7.5cm), the food will burn instead of cook properly.

5 Baste kababs with reserved marinade during grilling and just before serving. The marinade adds moistness as well as flavour. Use a long-handled pastry brush for brushing.

Ham and Apricot Kababs

8 ounces (225g) tinned pineapple chunks
6 ounces (175g) apricot preserves
2 tablespoons bottled steak sauce
1 tablespoon vinegar
¼ teaspoon ground cinnamon
1 pound (450g) ham, cooked
2 green peppers, cut into 1-inch (2.5cm) squares
2 tablespoons apricot preserves

Drain pineapple, reserving syrup. For marinade, in a bowl stir together reserved pineapple syrup, 6 ounces (175g) apricot preserves, steak sauce, vinegar, and cinnamon.

Cut ham into 1-inch (2.5cm) cubes. For the kababs, thread ham alternately with pineapple and green peppers onto eight 9-inch (23cm) wooden skewers. Place kababs in a shallow dish. Pour marinade over kababs. Cover and marinate 20 minutes at room temperature or 8 to 24 hours in the refrigerator; turn kababs several times.

Preheat the grill. Drain kababs and reserve marinade. Place kababs on the *unheated* rack of a grill pan. Place kababs 3 to 4 inches (7.5 to 10cm) from the heat (see photo 4, page 87). Grill for 5 minutes. Brush kababs with reserved marinade (see photo 5, page 87). Turn kababs and brush again with marinade. Grill 5 minutes more. Stir together *2 tablespoons* of remaining marinade and 2 tablespoons apricot preserves; brush over kababs before serving. Serves 4.

Assembling time: 30 minutes
Marinating time: 20 minutes to 24 hours
Cooking time: 10 minutes

Meat and Potato Kababs

A different twist for meat and potato lovers.

1 pound (450g) boneless sirloin steak *or* boneless lamb
4 fluid ounces (110ml) cooking oil
3 fluid ounces (80ml) soy sauce
2 fluid ounces (55ml) lemon juice
1 to 2 tablespoons prepared mustard
1 to 2 tablespoons Worcestershire sauce
¼ teaspoon pepper
⅛ teaspoon garlic powder
2 small onions
16 ounces (450g) tinned whole new potatoes, drained
Paprika (optional)

Cut steak or lamb into 1-inch (2.5cm) cubes. For the marinade, in a bowl stir together oil, soy sauce, lemon juice, mustard, Worcestershire sauce, pepper, and garlic powder. Add meat, then stir to coat well. Cover and marinate 20 minutes at room temperature or 8 to 24 hours in the refrigerator; stir occasionally.

Preheat the grill. Meanwhile, cut onions into wedges. Drain meat and reserve marinade. For the kababs, thread meat alternately with onion wedges and potatoes onto eight 8- or 9-inch (20 or 23cm) skewers.

Place kababs on the *unheated* rack of a grill pan. Brush kababs with reserved marinade. Place kababs 3 to 4 inches (7.5 to 10cm) from the heat (see photo 4, page 87). Grill for 5 minutes. Brush kababs with marinade (see photo 5, page 87). Carefully turn kababs and brush again with marinade. Grill 6 to 8 minutes more or until meat is desired doneness. Sprinkle potatoes with paprika, if desired. Makes 4 servings.

Assembling time: 15 minutes
Marinating time: 20 minutes to 24 hours
Cooking time: 11 to 13 minutes

Italian Chicken Kababs

The simple and quick Italian salad dressing marinade adds lots of zippy flavour.

1¼	pounds (550g) boneless, skinned chicken breasts
5	fluid ounces (140ml) Italian salad dressing
2	tablespoons lemon juice
1	medium green pepper
12	large mushroom caps
	Paprika (optional)

Cut chicken into strips (see photo 1, page 86). For marinade, in a bowl stir together Italian salad dressing and lemon juice. Add chicken strips, then stir to coat well. Cover and marinate 20 to 30 minutes at room temperature.

Meanwhile, cut the green pepper into 1-inch (2.5cm) squares. Pour *boiling water* over green pepper squares and mushroom caps; let stand 1 to 2 minutes. Drain the pepper squares and mushrooms. Drain the chicken and reserve the marinade.

Preheat the grill. For the kababs, thread chicken strips alternately with mushrooms and green pepper onto eight 8- or 9-inch (20 to 23cm) skewers (see photo 3, page 87).

Place kababs on the *unheated* rack of a grill pan. Place kababs 3 to 4 inches (7.5 to 10cm) from the heat (see photo 4, page 87). Grill for 5 minutes. Brush chicken with reserved marinade (see photo 5, page 87). Turn kababs and grill 5 to 6 minutes more or until chicken is done. Brush again with marinade. If desired, sprinkle kababs with paprika before serving. Makes 4 servings.

Assembling time: 15 minutes
Marinating time: 20 to 30 minutes
Cooking time: 10 to 11 minutes

Spicy Pork Kababs

Skewer fruit and pork together for a flavour-winning combination.

1	pound (450g) boneless pork
8	ounces (225g) tinned pineapple chunks in juice
1	small onion, finely chopped
3	tablespoons soy sauce
1	tablespoon soft brown sugar
1	tablespoon lemon juice
1	tablespoon cooking oil
1	teaspoon ground coriander
1	teaspoon ground cumin
⅛	teaspoon ground red pepper
1	clove garlic, minced
1	medium courgette, cut into ¼-inch (.5cm) slices
1	apple, cut into ¼-inch (.5cm) wedges
	Hot cooked rice (optional)

Cut pork into 1-inch (2.5cm) cubes. Drain pineapple, reserving 2 fluid ounces (55ml) juice. For marinade, in a bowl stir together reserved pineapple juice, onion, soy sauce, brown sugar, lemon juice, oil, coriander, cumin, red pepper, and garlic. Add meat to marinade, then stir to coat well. Cover and marinate 20 minutes at room temperature or 8 to 24 hours in the refrigerator; stir occasionally.

Preheat the grill. Drain meat and reserve marinade. For the kababs, thread meat alternately with courgette, apple, and pineapple onto eight 8- or 9-inch (20 to 23cm) skewers.

Place kababs on the *unheated* rack of a grill pan. Brush kababs with reserved marinade. Place kababs 3 to 4 inches (7.5 to 10cm) from the heat (see photo 4, page 87). Grill for 8 minutes. Carefully turn kababs and brush again with marinade (see photo 5, page 87). Grill 7 to 8 minutes more or until pork is done. Brush with any additional marinade before serving. Serve with rice, if desired. Makes 4 servings.

Assembling time: 25 minutes
Marinating time: 20 minutes to 24 hours
Cooking time: 15 to 16 minutes

Convenient Quiches

Forget pastry-making forever! With our shortcut quiches, you can skip the pastry-making part.

The luscious quiche you see here starts with purchased, rolled-out pastry. Or, try a mock pastry case made with pasta or stuffing mix for other quiches. Sound simple?

The fillings are just as easy and they're deliciously different.

Hearty Italian Quiche

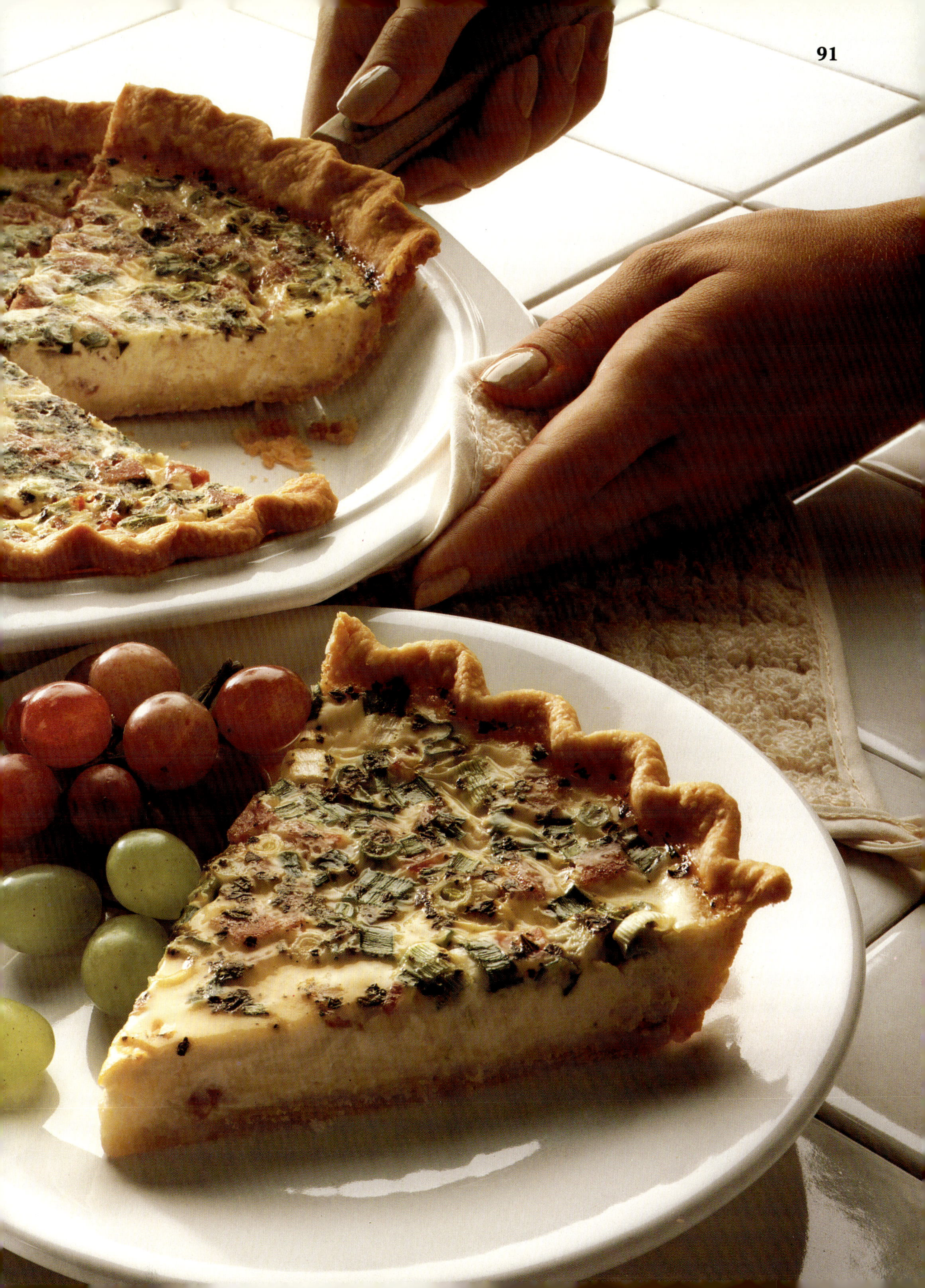

- 12 ounces (350g) frozen *or* fresh uncooked pastry
- 3 eggs
- 12 fluid ounces (330ml) milk
- 4 spring onions, thinly sliced
- ½ teaspoon dried oregano, crushed
- 4 ounces (110g) grated mozzarella cheese
- 1 tablespoon plain flour
- 3 ounces (75g) salami

Thaw pastry if necessary. Roll out the pastry to ⅛-inch (3mm) thick; line a 9-inch (23cm) pie dish. Press foil into the pie dish (see photo 1). Remove the foil.

Place foil "shell" atop pastry case (see photo 2). Bake in a 450°F (230°C) gas mark 8 oven for 5 minutes. Carefully remove foil; bake for 5 minutes more. Remove from oven. Reduce the oven temperature to 325°F (170°C) gas mark 3.

Meanwhile, in a mixing bowl slightly beat eggs with a rotary whisk or wire whisk. Stir in milk, onion, and oregano. Toss together cheese and flour (see photo 3). Chop salami. Stir cheese mixture and salami into egg mixture. Pour into hot pastry case (see photo 4). Bake in a 325°F (170°C) gas mark 3 oven for 35 to 40 minutes or until done (see photo 5). Let stand 10 minutes. Makes 6 servings.

Assembling time: 30 minutes
Cooking time: 35 to 40 minutes
Standing time: 10 minutes

1 Press a double thickness of heavy-duty foil into a 9-inch (23cm) pie dish. Mould foil to the shape of a pie dish. Carefully remove the foil "shell," keeping it in the pie-dish shape.

2 Transfer pastry to the pie dish. Place the foil "shell" atop. Gently press foil against the pastry. The foil helps prevent the pastry from puffing and shrinking during baking.

3 Toss the grated cheese and the flour together to get the flour evenly distributed. If you do this on a piece of greaseproof paper there will be no bowl to wash!

4 Remove prebaked pastry case from oven and immediately pour filling into the hot case. Prebaking the case and adding filling to the hot pastry helps prevent soggy bottomed pastry.

5 To test if the quiche is cooked through, insert a knife near the centre of the pie. It should come out clean, as shown. If it doesn't test done (some egg mixture remains on knife), bake about 5 minutes longer. Let quiche stand 10 minutes before serving—it will set up more so it'll hold a firmer edge when cut.

Three-Cheese Quiche

Use your blender or food processor to make a smooth cheese filling in no time.

- 12 ounces (350g) frozen *or* fresh uncooked pastry
- 3 eggs
- 4 ounces (110g) grated cheddar cheese
- 4 ounces (110g) cottage cheese
- 1 ounce (25g) grated Parmesan cheese
- 1 tablespoon plain flour
- ¼ teaspoon ground red pepper
- 11 fluid ounces (300ml) milk
- 1½ ounces (40g) prepared fried onions

Thaw pastry if necessary. Roll out to ⅛-inch (3mm) thick; line 9-inch (23cm) pie dish. Press foil into the pie dish (see photo 1, page 92). Remove the foil.

Place foil "shell" atop pastry case (see photo 2, page 92). Bake in a 450°F (230°C) gas mark 8 oven for 5 minutes. Carefully remove foil; bake for 5 minutes more. Remove from oven. Reduce oven temperature to 325°F (170°C) gas mark 3.

Meanwhile, in a blender or food processor bowl combine eggs, cheddar cheese, cottage cheese, Parmesan cheese, flour, and pepper. Cover; blend or process until smooth. Pour into a mixing bowl. Stir in milk. Pour into hot pastry case (see photo 4, page 93). Bake in a 325°F (170°C) gas mark 3 oven for 40 to 45 minutes or until done (see photo 5, page 93). Sprinkle onions atop. Let stand 10 minutes. Makes 6 servings.

Assembling time: 30 minutes
Cooking time: 40 to 45 minutes
Standing time: 10 minutes

Quiche in Pasta Crust

The egg that's mixed with the linguine helps the pasta hold its pastry case shape.

- 6 ounces (175g) linguine *or* spaghetti
- 2 eggs
- 1½ ounces (40g) grated Parmesan cheese
- 1 tablespoon butter *or* margarine, melted
- 6 ounces (175g) grated Swiss cheese
- 2 eggs
- 8 fluid ounces (220ml) milk
- 1 teaspoon minced dried onion
- ⅛ teaspoon salt
- ⅛ teaspoon garlic powder
- 1 tablespoon plain flour
- 3 tablespoons cooked bacon pieces *or* 4 rashers streaky bacon, crisp-cooked, drained, and crumbled

Cook linguine or spaghetti according to the packet directions. Drain well. In a mixing bowl beat 2 eggs with a rotary or wire whisk. Stir in Parmesan cheese and butter or margarine. Toss the drained pasta with the egg mixture until well coated.

Press pasta mixture onto bottom and up sides of a well-greased 10-inch (25.5cm) quiche dish or pie dish to form a "crust." Sprinkle *4 ounces (110g)* of the Swiss cheese over crust.

In a mixing bowl slightly beat 2 eggs with a rotary whisk or wire whisk. Stir in milk, onion, salt, and garlic powder. Toss together remaining Swiss cheese and flour (see photo 3, page 93). Stir cheese mixture and bacon into egg mixture. Pour into crust. Bake in a 325°F (170°C) gas mark 3 oven for 30 to 40 minutes or until done (see photo 5, page 93). Let stand 10 minutes. Makes 6 servings.

Assembling time: 30 minutes
Cooking time: 30 to 40 minutes
Standing time: 10 minutes

Turkey Quiche

If you're tired of making sandwiches from leftover turkey, here's a great way to use up some of the extra!

- 6 ounces (175g) sage and onion stuffing mix
- 4 eggs
- 5 fluid ounces (140ml) evaporated milk
- ⅛ teaspoon dried tarragon, crushed
- Dash pepper
- 6 ounces (175g) grated Swiss cheese
- 1 tablespoon plain flour
- 6 ounces (175g) chopped cooked turkey *or* chicken

Prepare stuffing mix according to packet directions. Press evenly onto bottom and up sides of a 9-inch (23cm) pie dish to form a crust. Bake in a 400°F (200°C) gas mark 6 oven for 10 minutes. Remove from oven. Reduce the oven temperature to 325°F (170°C) gas mark 3.

Meanwhile, in a mixing bowl slightly beat eggs with a rotary whisk or wire whisk. Stir in milk, tarragon, and pepper. Toss together cheese and flour (see photo 3, page 93). Stir cheese mixture and turkey or chicken into egg mixture. Pour into hot crust (see photo 4, page 93). Bake in a 325°F (170°C) gas mark 3 oven about 40 minutes or until done (see photo 5, page 93). Let stand 10 minutes. Makes 6 servings.

Assembling time: 20 minutes
Cooking time: 40 minutes
Standing time: 10 minutes

Ham and Potato Quiche

- 4 fluid ounces (110ml) water
- 2 ounces (50g) butter *or* margarine
- 6 ounces (175g) sage and onion stuffing mix
- 2 ounces (50g) loose-pack frozen potato chunks
- 4 eggs
- 5 fluid ounces (140ml) evaporated milk
- 2 teaspoons minced dried onion
- 5 ounces (150g) grated cheddar cheese
- 1 tablespoon plain flour
- 2 ounces (50g) diced cooked ham

In a saucepan heat water and butter or margarine until butter is melted. Stir in stuffing mix. Press evenly onto bottom and up sides of a greased 9-inch (23cm) pie dish to form a crust. Bake in a 400°F (200°C) gas mark 6 oven for 15 minutes. Remove from oven. Reduce oven temperature to 325°F (170°C) gas mark 3.

Meanwhile, place potatoes in a sieve or colander. Run warm water over hash browns for 30 seconds or until thawed. Set aside.

In a mixing bowl slightly beat eggs with a rotary or wire whisk. Stir in milk and onion. Toss together *4 ounces (110g)* of the cheese and flour (see photo 3, page 93). Stir potatoes, cheese mixture, and ham into egg mixture. Pour into hot crust (see photo 4, page 93). Bake in a 325°F (170°C) gas mark 3 oven about 35 minutes or until done (see photo 5, page 93). Sprinkle with remaining cheese. Let stand 10 minutes. Makes 6 servings.

Assembling time: 25 minutes
Cooking time: 35 minutes
Standing time: 10 minutes

Sensational Stir-Frys

It's no wonder that stir-frying is the most popular Oriental cooking method. It's so quick and easy!

Give stir-frying a try for supper tonight. You don't even need a wok—a large frying pan works just as well. Once you've mastered the stir-frying technique, you'll discover countless meat and vegetable combinations you can toss together.

Scallops and Mange Tout

98 Sensational Stir-Frys

Scallops and Mange Tout

12	ounces (350g) fresh *or* frozen scallops
6	ounces (175g) frozen mange tout
1	small onion
8	cherry tomatoes
3	fluid ounces (80ml) sake *or* dry sherry
2	fluid ounces (55ml) cold water
2	teaspoons cornflour
1	teaspoon instant chicken bouillon granules
1	teaspoon caster sugar
1	teaspoon soy sauce
1	teaspoon grated root ginger *or* ¼ teaspoon ground ginger
2	tablespoons cooking oil
	Hot cooked rice

Thaw scallops, if frozen, by placing under running water (see photo 3, page 20). Drain well. Cut large scallops in half. Run warm water over frozen mange tout to thaw; drain well. Cut onion into slices and cherry tomatoes in half lengthwise; set aside. In a small bowl stir together sake or sherry, water, cornflour, bouillon granules, sugar, soy sauce, and root ginger or ground ginger (see photo 1). Set aside.

Preheat a wok or large frying pan over high heat; add *1 tablespoon* of oil (see photo 2). Add onion slices to the wok or frying pan. Stir-fry 1 to 2 minutes. Add mange tout, then stir-fry 1 to 2 minutes more or until the vegetables are crisp but tender (see photo 3). Transfer vegetables to a bowl.

Add remaining oil to the hot wok or frying pan. Add scallops; stir-fry 1 to 2 minutes or until done. Push scallops from centre of the wok. Stir cornflour mixture, then add to the centre of the wok or frying pan (see photo 4). Cook and stir until thickened and bubbly, then cook and stir 1 minute more. Stir in the vegetables. Place tomatoes atop vegetables. Cover and cook 1 to 2 minutes more or until heated through. Serve with rice. Makes 4 servings.

Assembling time: 15 minutes
Cooking time: 6 to 10 minutes

1 Stir-frying is such a quick-cooking process that you need to have all the ingredients ready before you begin. This includes stirring together the cornflour mixture. Cornflour settles on the bottom of the bowl as it sits. That's why the mixture must be stirred again just before it's added to the wok.

2 Place the wok over a burner set on high heat. When the wok is very hot, add the cooking oil in a ring around the upper part of the wok so it coats the sides as it runs to the centre of the wok, as shown. If you are using a frying pan, add the oil to the centre of the frying pan, then lift and tilt frying pan to coat the bottom with oil.

3 Add onion slices and begin stir-frying. Use a long-handled spoon or cooking spatula. Gently lift and turn the food with a folding motion so it cooks evenly. It's important to keep the food moving at all times, otherwise it will quickly burn. Add mange tout; stir-fry, as shown.

4 Push the cooked food away from the middle of the wok, leaving the centre clear of food. Stir cornflour mixture and add it to centre of the wok. Cook and stir until mixture is thickened and bubbly, then cook and stir 1 minute more. This ensures that the thickener is completely cooked.

Easy Chicken Stir-Fry

1 pound (450g) boneless, skinned chicken breasts
16 ounces loose-pack frozen French mixed vegetables, broccoli, mushrooms, and red pepper
6 fluid ounces (165ml) cold water
2 fluid ounces (55ml) soy sauce
1 tablespoon cornflour
½ teaspoon ground ginger
2 tablespoons cooking oil
Chow mein noodles

Cut chicken into thin bite-size strips. Run warm water over frozen vegetables until partially thawed (see photo 3, page 20). Drain well. In a small bowl stir together water, soy sauce, cornflour, and ginger (see photo 1, page 98). Set aside.

Preheat a wok or large frying pan over high heat; add *1 tablespoon* of oil (see photo 2, page 98). Add vegetables to the wok or frying pan. Stir-fry 2 minutes (see photo 3, page 99). Transfer vegetables to a bowl.

Add remaining oil to the hot wok or frying pan. Add *half* of the chicken to the wok or frying pan; stir-fry 2 to 3 minutes. Remove chicken. Stir-fry remaining chicken 2 to 3 minutes. Return all the chicken to the wok. Push chicken from centre.

Stir cornflour mixture, then add to the centre of the wok or frying pan (see photo 4, page 99). Cook and stir until thickened and bubbly, then cook and stir 1 minute more. Stir in vegetables. Cover and cook 1 minute more. Serve with chow mein noodles. Makes 6 servings.

Assembling time: 15 minutes
Cooking time: 9 to 11 minutes

Cranberry-Orange Turkey Stir-Fry

Serve this saucy mixture over fresh bean sprouts or rice, whichever you prefer. Both are delicious!

12 ounces (350g) boneless turkey breast slices *or* boneless, skinned chicken breasts
9 ounces (250g) frozen sliced green beans
8 ounces (225g) tinned cranberry sauce
2 fluid ounces (55ml) orange juice
3 tablespoons soy sauce
2 tablespoons cold water
4 teaspoons cornflour
2 tablespoons cooking oil
16 ounces (450g) fresh bean sprouts *or* 14 ounces (400g) hot cooked rice

Cut turkey or chicken into thin bite-size strips. Run warm water over frozen green beans to thaw (see photo 3, page 20). Drain well. In a small bowl combine cranberry sauce, orange juice, soy sauce, water, and cornflour. Mix ingredients together with a fork until combined (see photo 1, page 98). Set aside.

Preheat a wok or large frying pan over high heat; add *1 tablespoon* of oil (see photo 2, page 98). Add green beans to the wok or frying pan. Stir-fry 2 to 3 minutes (see photo 3, page 99). Transfer beans to bowl. Add remaining oil to the hot wok or frying pan. Add turkey or chicken; stir-fry 3 to 4 minutes. Push turkey or chicken from centre of the wok.

Stir cranberry mixture, then add to the centre of the wok or frying pan (see photo 4, page 99). Cook and stir until thickened and bubbly, then cook and stir 1 minute more. Stir in green beans. Cover and cook 1 minute more.

Place bean sprouts in colander; run hot tap water over sprouts until warmed. Serve cranberry-poultry mixture over bean sprouts or rice. Makes 4 servings.

Assembling time: 10 minutes
Cooking time: 8 to 10 minutes

Chicken Liver Stir-Fry

Add a crisp salad and a colourful vegetable to finish off this main dish.

5	ounces (150g) wide noodles
4	fluid ounces (110ml) chicken broth
2	fluid ounces (55ml) dry white wine
1	tablespoon cornflour
½	teaspoon dried thyme, crushed
¼	teaspoon salt
⅛	teaspoon garlic powder
1	large green pepper
1	small onion
12	ounces (350g) chicken livers
2	tablespoons cooking oil

Cook noodles according to the packet directions. Drain and keep warm. Meanwhile, in a bowl stir together broth, wine, cornflour, thyme, salt, and garlic powder (see photo 1, page 98). Set aside. Cut green pepper into 1-inch (2.5cm) squares. Cut onion into thin wedges. Cut large chicken livers in half.

Preheat a wok or large frying pan over high heat; add *1 tablespoon* of oil (see photo 2, page 98). Add green pepper and onion to the wok or frying pan, then stir-fry 1 to 2 minutes (see photo 3, page 99). Transfer vegetables to a bowl. Add remaining oil to the hot wok or frying pan. Add chicken livers to the wok or frying pan. Stir-fry 3 to 4 minutes or until just pink.

Push livers from centre of the wok. Stir cornflour mixture, then add to the centre of the wok or frying pan (see photo 4, page 99). Turn heat to medium-low. Cook and stir until thickened and bubbly. Stir in vegetables. Cover and cook 2 minutes more over low heat. Serve at once over noodles. Makes 4 servings.

Assembling time: 10 minutes
Cooking time: 12 minutes

No-Chop Prawn Stir-Fry

These frozen prawns and vegetables need no cutting—they're ready to use when you're ready to cook.

5	ounces (150g) long grain rice
12	ounces (350g) fresh *or* frozen shelled prawns
16	ounces (450g) loose-pack frozen broccoli mixed vegetables
4	fluid ounces (110ml) cold water
2	fluid ounces (55ml) soy sauce
2	fluid ounces (55ml) dry sherry
1	tablespoon cornflour
¼	teaspoon crushed red pepper
⅛	teaspoon garlic powder
2	tablespoons cooking oil
2	ounces (50g) peanuts

Prepare rice according to the packet directions. Meanwhile, thaw prawns, if frozen, by placing under running water (see photo 3, page 20). Drain well. Run warm water over frozen vegetables until partially thawed; drain well.

In a small bowl stir together cold water, soy sauce, sherry, cornflour, red pepper, and garlic powder (see photo 1, page 98). Set aside.

Preheat a wok or large frying pan over high heat; add *1 tablespoon* of oil (see photo 2, page 98). Add partially thawed vegetables to the wok or frying pan. Stir-fry 2 to 3 minutes or until vegetables are just tender (see photo 3, page 99). Transfer vegetables to a bowl.

Add remaining oil to the hot wok or frying pan. Add prawns; stir-fry 3 to 5 minutes or until prawns turn pink. Push prawns from the centre of the wok. Stir cornflour mixture, then add to the centre of the wok or frying pan (see photo 4, page 99). Cook and stir until thickened and bubbly, then cook and stir 1 minute more. Stir in the vegetables and peanuts. Cover and cook about 1 minute more or until heated through. Serve the prawn-vegetable mixture with hot rice. Makes 4 servings.

Assembling time: 10 minutes
Cooking time: 20 minutes

Ham and Pecan Stir-Fry

8	ounces (225g) tinned pineapple chunks in juice
¾	pound (350g) ham, fully cooked
1	medium green pepper
2	tablespoons soy sauce
2	tablespoons dry sherry
2	teaspoons cornflour
¼	to ½ teaspoon crushed red pepper
2	tablespoons cooking oil
2	ounces (50g) walnut *or* pecan halves
	Hot cooked rice

Drain pineapple, reserving juice. Cut ham into bite-size strips. Cut green pepper into 1-inch (2.5cm) pieces. In a small bowl stir together reserved pineapple juice, soy sauce, sherry, cornflour, and red pepper (see photo 1, page 98). Set the mixture aside.

Preheat a wok or large frying pan over high heat; add *1 tablespoon* of oil (see photo 2, page 98). Add walnuts or pecans to the wok or frying pan. Stir-fry 30 seconds or until toasted; remove from wok. Add green pepper, then stir-fry 1 minute (see photo 3, page 99). Transfer green pepper to a bowl.

Add remaining oil to the hot wok or frying pan. Add ham; stir-fry 2 minutes. Push ham from centre of the wok. Stir cornflour mixture, then add to the centre of the wok or frying pan (see photo 4, page 99). Cook and stir until thickened and bubbly, then cook and stir 1 minute more. Stir in green pepper, pineapple, and walnuts or pecans. Cover and cook 1 to 2 minutes more or until heated through. Serve with rice. Makes 4 servings.

Assembling time: 15 minutes
Cooking time: 7 to 8 minutes

Teriyaki-Sauced Beef And Courgettes

¾	pound (350g) beef top-side
2	medium courgettes
2	fluid ounces (55ml) bottled teriyaki sauce
2	tablespoons orange juice
2	teaspoons cornflour
1	teaspoon minced dried onion
2	tablespoons cooking oil
	Hot cooked rice

Cut beef into bite-size strips. Thinly slice courgettes. In a small bowl stir together teriyaki sauce, orange juice, cornflour, and onion (see photo 1, page 98). Set aside.

Preheat a wok or large frying pan over high heat; add *1 tablespoon* of oil (see photo 2, page 98). Add courgettes to the wok or frying pan. Stir-fry 1 minute (see photo 3, page 99). Transfer courgettes to a bowl.

Add remaining oil to the hot wok or frying pan. Add beef; stir-fry 2 to 3 minutes. Push beef from the centre. Stir cornflour mixture, then add to the centre of the wok or frying pan (see photo 4, page 99). Cook and stir until thickened and bubbly, then cook and stir 1 minute more. Stir in courgettes. Cover and cook 1 to 2 minutes more or until heated through. Serve over rice. Serves 4.

Assembling time: 20 minutes
Cooking time: 6 to 8 minutes

Mustard-Sauced Liver

1 pound (450g) ox liver
8 ounces (225g) broccoli
2 fluid ounces (55ml) cold water
2 tablespoons soy sauce
1 tablespoon dry mustard
1½ teaspoons cornflour
1 teaspoon caster sugar
½ teaspoon instant beef bouillon granules
⅛ teaspoon onion powder *or* dried onion flakes
3 tablespoons cooking oil
1 medium tomato, cut into wedges
Chow mein noodles

Cut liver into bite-size pieces. Cut broccoli into ½-inch (1cm) pieces. In a small bowl stir together water, soy sauce, dry mustard, cornflour, sugar, bouillon granules, and onion powder (see photo 1, page 98). Set aside.

Preheat a wok or large frying pan over high heat; add *1 tablespoon* of oil (see photo 2, page 98). Add broccoli to the wok or frying pan. Stir-fry 3 minutes (see photo 3, page 99). Transfer broccoli to a bowl.

Add another tablespoon of oil to the hot wok or frying pan. Add *half* of the liver; stir-fry 2 to 3 minutes or until liver is done. Remove liver. Add remaining oil. Stir-fry remaining liver 2 to 3 minutes. Return all liver to wok. Push liver from centre of the wok.

Stir cornflour mixture, then add to the centre of the wok or frying pan (see photo 4, page 99). Cook and stir until thickened and bubbly, then cook and stir 30 seconds more. Stir broccoli and tomato into liver mixture. Cover and cook 1 to 2 minutes more or until heated through. Serve over chow mein noodles. Serves 6.

Assembling time: 15 minutes
Cooking time: 10 to 13 minutes

Sausage-Onion Stir-Fry

German sausage, lots of onion, and bulgur or noodles make this a robust main dish.

1 pound (450g) cooked German sausage
3 medium onions
10 ounces (275g) frozen cauliflower
4 fluid ounces (110ml) cold water
3 fluid ounces (80ml) dry sherry
2 tablespoons soy sauce
1 tablespoon cornflour
⅛ teaspoon garlic powder
⅛ teaspoon pepper
1 tablespoon cooking oil
Hot cooked bulgur *or* noodles

Cut sausage into ¼-inch (.5cm) slices. Cut onions into thin wedges. Run warm water over frozen cauliflower to thaw (see photo 3, page 20). Drain well. Cut up any large pieces. In a small bowl stir together water, sherry, soy sauce, cornflour, garlic powder, and pepper (see photo 1, page 98). Set aside.

Preheat a wok or large frying pan over high heat; add cooking oil (see photo 2, page 98). Add onions to the wok or frying pan. Stir-fry 3 minutes. Add cauliflower and stir-fry 3 to 4 minutes more or until onions and cauliflower are tender (see photo 3, page 99). Transfer the vegetables to a bowl.

Add sausage to wok and stir-fry 2 minutes. Push sausage from the centre of the wok. Stir cornflour mixture, then add to the centre of the wok or frying pan (see photo 4, page 99). Cook and stir until thickened and bubbly, then cook and stir 1 minute more. Stir in vegetables. Cover and cook 1 minute more or until heated through. Serve over bulgur or noodles. Makes 4 servings.

Assembling time: 15 minutes
Cooking time: 11 to 12 minutes

Skip-a-Step Pasta

Luscious lasagne and marvellous cannelloni dishes finally have been simplified just for you, the busy cook.

Skip the time-consuming steps of cooking the pasta and sauce separately. Instead, bake all the ingredients together in a single dish. The results are fantastic!

Courgette Lasagne

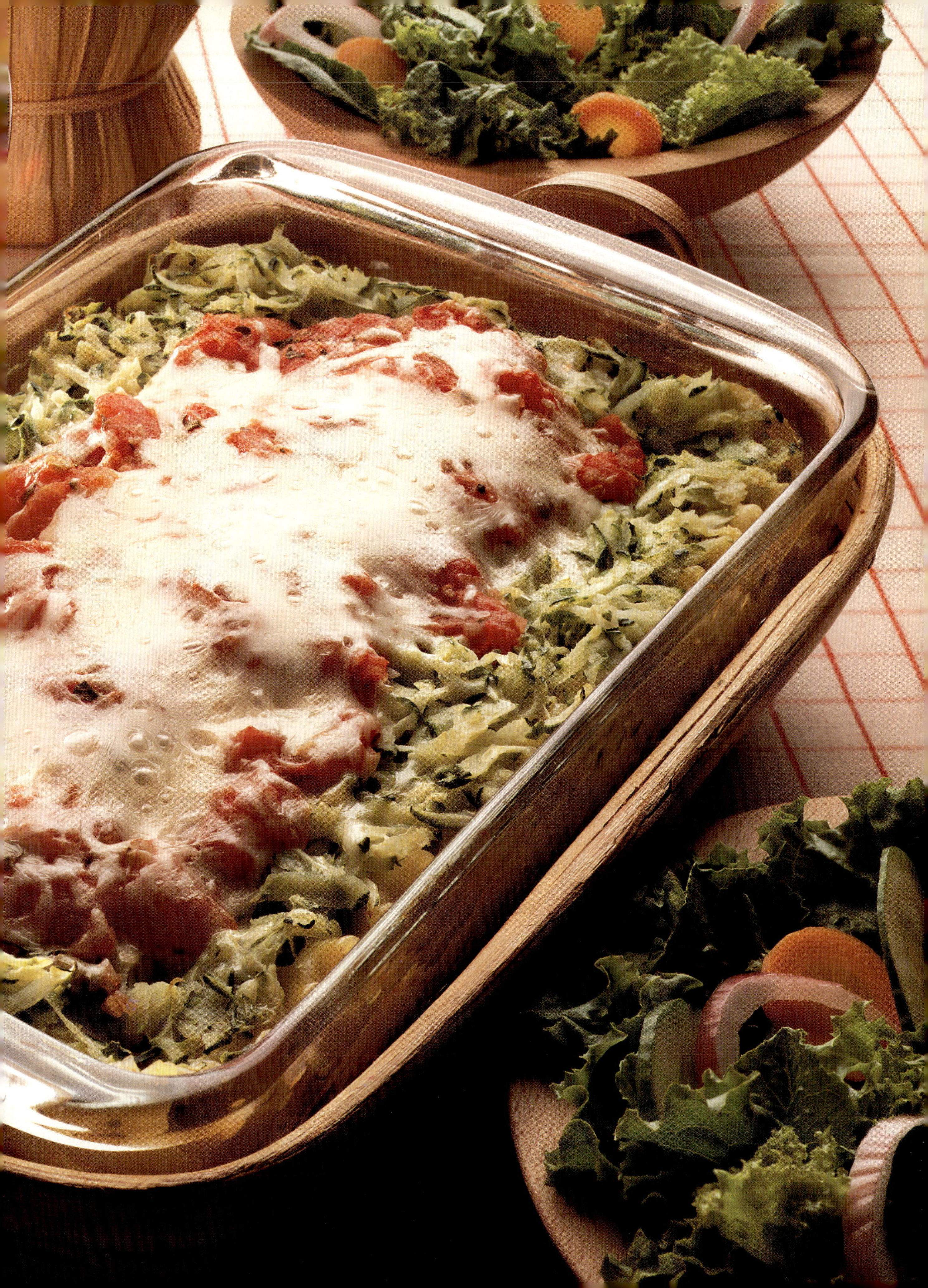

Courgette Lasagne

- 8 ounces (225g) ricotta cheese
- 1 egg
- 4 ounces (110g) grated mozzarella cheese
- 1 ounce (25g) grated Parmesan cheese
- 14 ounces (400g) tinned chopped tomatoes
- 1 tablespoon cornflour
- 1 tablespoon minced dried onion
- 1 teaspoon dried oregano, crushed
- 6 lasagne strips
- 8 ounces (225g) shredded courgette (about 1½ medium courgettes)
- 2 ounces (50g) grated mozzarella cheese
- 5 fluid ounces (145ml) boiling water

In a mixing bowl stir together ricotta cheese and egg. Stir in 4 ounces (110g) mozzarella cheese and Parmesan cheese. Stir together *undrained* tomatoes, cornflour, onion, and oregano.

Place *2* of the *uncooked* lasagne strips in a 10x6x2-inch (25.5x15x5cm) baking dish (see photo 1). Layer with *half* of the tomato mixture. Arrange *2* more *uncooked* lasagne in the dish. Spread ricotta mixture atop (see photo 2). Top with remaining lasagne, courgette, and remaining tomato mixture. Sprinkle with 2 ounces (50g) mozzarella cheese.

Slowly pour boiling water into the dish around the entire inside edge (see photo 3). Cover tightly with foil. Bake in a 350°F (180°C) gas mark 4 oven for 60 to 65 minutes or until done (see photo 4). Let stand, covered, for 10 minutes. Makes 6 servings.

Assembling time: 20 minutes
Cooking time: 60 to 65 minutes
Standing time: 10 minutes

1 Lay two lasagne strips, side by side, in the bottom of the baking dish. You may need to break a piece off each strip so it fits neatly in the baking dish.

2 Spread all of the ricotta mixture over the second layer of uncooked lasagne. Use a rubber spatula to help spread the mixture.

3 Make a little "ditch" around the lasagne mixture along the edge of the baking dish. Then, carefully pour boiling water into this "ditch." The water is essential for cooking the pasta properly.

4 To test if the lasagne is done, either prick a strip or drag a fork across one to see if it is tender. Re-cover dish, then let mixture stand so it holds a better cut edge.

Spaghetti Sauce Lasagne

15½ ounces (440g) tinned spaghetti sauce with meat
¾ teaspoon dried basil, crushed
⅛ teaspoon garlic powder
2 eggs
12 ounces (350g) cottage cheese, drained
1 ounce (25g) grated Parmesan cheese
1 tablespoon dried parsley
¼ teaspoon pepper
⅛ teaspoon salt
6 lasagne strips
6 ounces (175g) grated mozzarella cheese
4 fluid ounces (110ml) boiling water

Combine spaghetti sauce, basil, and garlic powder; set aside. In a mixing bowl slightly beat eggs. Stir in cottage cheese, Parmesan cheese, parsley, pepper, and salt.

Place *2* of the *uncooked* lasagne strips in a 10x6x2-inch (25.5x15x5cm) baking dish (see photo 1, page 106). Layer with *one-third* of the spaghetti sauce mixture, *half* of the cottage cheese mixture, and *2 ounces (50g)* mozzarella cheese. Repeat the layers of *uncooked* lasagne, spaghetti sauce mixture, cottage cheese mixture, and mozzarella cheese. Top with remaining lasagne, spaghetti sauce mixture, and mozzarella cheese.

Slowly pour boiling water into dish around the entire inside edge (see photo 3, page 107). Cover tightly with foil. Bake in a 350°F (180°C) gas mark 4 oven for 60 to 65 minutes or until done (see photo 4, page 107). Let stand, covered, for 10 minutes. Serves 6.

Assembling time: 20 minutes
Cooking time: 60 to 65 minutes
Standing time: 10 minutes

Chicken Lasagne

Gone are the days when lasagne strips come in just one flavour—choose either whole wheat or spinach noodles for variety.

8 ounces (225g) cottage cheese
3 ounces (75g) cream cheese, softened and cut up
11 fluid ounces (325ml) tinned condensed cream of mushroom soup
8 ounces (225g) loose-pack frozen cut broccoli
2 ounces (50g) sliced celery
2 fluid ounces (55ml) milk
1 teaspoon minced dried onion
¼ teaspoon dried oregano, crushed
⅛ teaspoon ground sage
6 lasagne strips
6 ounces (175g) chopped cooked chicken *or* turkey
2 ounces (50g) grated cheddar cheese
5 fluid ounces (140ml) boiling water

In a mixing bowl stir together cottage cheese and cream cheese; set aside. In a mixing bowl combine soup, broccoli, celery, milk, dried onion, oregano, and sage; set aside.

Place *2* of the *uncooked* lasagne strips in a 10x6x2-inch (25.5x15x5cm) baking dish (see photo 1, page 106). Layer with *half* of the cottage cheese mixture and *one-third* of the soup mixture. Repeat layers of lasagne, cottage cheese mixture, and soup mixture. Top with remaining lasagne, chicken or turkey, and remaining soup mixture. Sprinkle with cheddar cheese.

Slowly pour boiling water into dish around the entire inside edge (see photo 3, page 107). Cover tightly with foil. Bake in a 350°F (180°C) gas mark 4 oven for 60 to 65 minutes or until done (see photo 4, page 107). Let stand, covered, for 10 minutes. Serves 6.

Assembling time: 25 minutes
Cooking time: 60 to 65 minutes
Standing time: 10 minutes

Mexican Cannelloni

10	frankfurters (1 pound [450g])
10	cannelloni shells
4	fluid ounces (110ml) boiling water
30	ounces (850g) tinned chilli con carne
8	fluid ounces (220ml) taco sauce
4	ounces (110g) grated cheddar cheese

Place *1* frankfurter in *each uncooked* cannelloni shell. Place the filled shells, so they are not touching, in a 12x7½x2-inch (30x19x5cm) baking dish. Slowly pour boiling water into the dish around the entire inside edge (see photo 3, page 107).

Stir together chilli and taco sauce. Spoon atop the filled shells. Sprinkle with cheese. Cover tightly with foil. Bake in a 350°F (180°C) gas mark 4 oven for 60 to 65 minutes or until shells are done (see photo 4, page 107). Let stand, covered, for 10 minutes. Makes 6 servings.

Assembling time: 15 minutes
Cooking time: 60 to 65 minutes
Standing time: 10 minutes

Pizza Cannelloni

¾	pound (350g) minced beef
1	small onion, chopped
¾	pint (425ml) pizza sauce
⅛	teaspoon garlic powder
	Dash pepper
4	ounces (110g) grated mozzarella *or* Gouda cheese
8	cannelloni shells
½	pint (275ml) boiling water
2	tablespoons sliced stoned black olives

In a 10-inch (25.5cm) frying pan cook beef and onion until meat is brown and onion is tender. Drain off fat. Stir 2 *fluid ounces (55ml)* pizza sauce, garlic powder, and pepper into meat mixture. Bring to the boil. Reduce heat, then simmer 5 minutes. Stir in cheese until melted. Let cool 5 minutes. Spoon mixture into *uncooked* cannelloni shells.

Place shells in a 10x6x2-inch (25x15x5cm) baking dish so they are not touching each other. Slowly pour boiling water into the dish around the entire inside edge (see photo 3, page 107). Reserve *4 fluid ounces (110ml)* pizza sauce. Pour the remaining sauce over shells, spreading to cover shells. Cover tightly with foil. Bake in a 350°F (180°C) gas mark 4 oven for 60 to 65 minutes or until shells are done (see photo 4, page 107). Let stand, covered, for 10 minutes.

Meanwhile, in a small saucepan heat reserved pizza sauce. Pour over cannelloni. Sprinkle with olives. Makes 4 servings.

Assembling time: 25 minutes
Cooking time: 60 to 65 minutes
Standing time: 10 minutes

Fix-and-Forget Oven Meals

Does taking some time off while preparing a meal sound appealing? Well, here's the secret. Just bake several dishes together in the oven. Once they're cooking, take it easy while the food looks after itself. Just follow our timetable on page 114 for the menu preparation steps. Another secret—make clearing up easier by using an oven cooking bag to roast the chicken.

Menu

- Lemon-Herbed Chicken
- Baked Squash with Peas
- Tossed salad
- Rolls and butter
- Deep-Dish Apple Pie

*see pages 112-115

*Lemon-Herbed Chicken
Baked Squash with Peas
Deep-Dish Apple Pie*

Lemon-Herbed Chicken

- 2 tablespoons butter *or* margarine
- 3 tablespoons lemon juice
- 1½ teaspoons dried rosemary *or* tarragon, crushed
- 1 3-pound (1kg350g) chicken
  Garlic salt
- 1 tablespoon plain flour
  Oven cooking bag

Melt butter or margarine. Stir lemon juice and rosemary or tarragon into melted butter or margarine. If desired, tie legs of chicken together and twist wings under back. Sprinkle chicken with garlic salt.

Sprinkle flour in the oven cooking bag according to packet directions. Place chicken in prepared bag. Pour in lemon-butter mixture (see photo 1). Close bag. Turn bag to coat chicken with lemon-butter mixture (see photo 2).

Place cooking bag with chicken, breast side up, in a 10x6x2-inch (25.5x15x5cm) baking dish. Cut slits in top of bag according to packet directions (see photo 3). Place chicken in a 375°F (190°C) gas mark 5 oven (see photo 4). Bake for 65 to 70 minutes or until done. Remove chicken from bag and transfer to a serving dish (see photo 5). Discard juices and cooking bag. Makes 6 servings.

Assembling time: 15 minutes
Cooking time: 65 to 70 minutes

1 Sprinkle flour in the oven cooking bag to prevent bag from bursting. Place chicken in the prepared bag, then pour the herbed butter mixture over the chicken.

2 Close bag using the closure included in the oven cooking bag packet. Turn bag with both hands, coating the entire chicken with the herbed butter mixture so the whole chicken is flavoured.

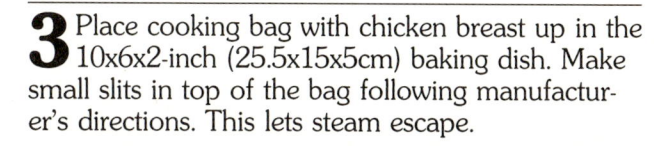

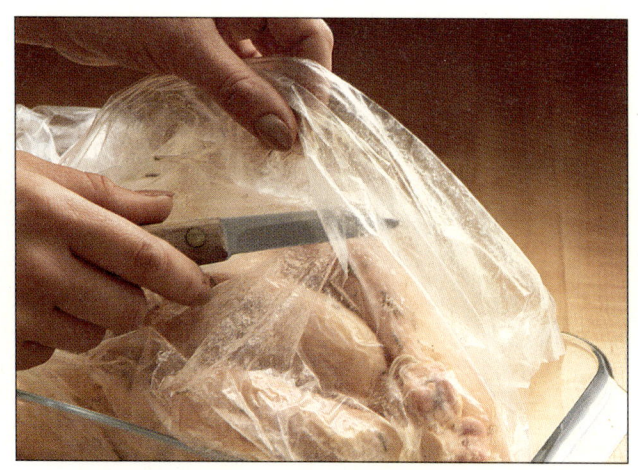

3 Place cooking bag with chicken breast up in the 10x6x2-inch (25.5x15x5cm) baking dish. Make small slits in top of the bag following manufacturer's directions. This lets steam escape.

4 The chicken is the longest cooking item for the menu, so add it to the oven first. Place it to one side of the oven, leaving space for the other dishes you want to include in your oven meal.

5 At serving time, carefully remove chicken from the cooking bag with a fork and wide spatula; transfer the bird to a serving dish. Use the spatula under the chicken and a fork to help you lift it to the dish.

114 Fix-and-Forget Oven Meals

Timetable

1¾ hrs. before
- Remove the pastry from the refrigerator or freezer. Stir together filling for the pie. Cut squash for Baked Squash with Peas, as shown. Place on the baking tray.
- Get the Lemon-Herbed Chicken ready for the oven, then set it aside. Prepare salad; cover the salad with dampened kitchen paper to keep it crisp. Place in refrigerator to chill.

70 min. before
- Set chicken into a preheated 375°F (190°C) gas mark 5 oven, placing dish to one side of the oven. Complete the apple pie, up to the baking step; flute pastry case to the sides of the dish as shown.

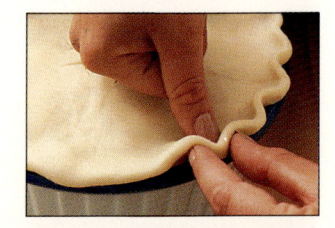

60 min. before
- Arrange the apple pie and the baking tray with the squash halves in the oven on the same rack as the chicken.

At Serving Time
- Cook the frozen peas and onions for the squash filling. Remove chicken, squash, and dessert from the oven. Transfer chicken to a serving plate, as shown. Fill squash halves with cooked peas and onions; place on the serving plate. Toss dressing and salad together. Place rolls in basket.

Baked Squash with Peas

- 3 small acorn squash (about 14 ounces [400g] each) *or* medium marrow
- Salt
- Pepper
- 6 ounces (175g) frozen peas
- 4 ounces (110g) frozen pearl onions

Split squash in half using a heavy knife. Remove and discard seeds from squash halves. Sprinkle inside of squash halves with salt and pepper.

Place the squash halves, cut side down, on a 13x9x2-inch (32.5x23x5cm) baking tray. Bake in a 375°F (190°C) gas mark 5 oven for 55 to 60 minutes or until squash is done.

About 10 minutes before serving, cook peas and onions according to packet directions. To serve, spoon hot peas and onions into squash halves. Makes 6 servings.

Assembling time: 10 minutes
Cooking time: 55 to 60 minutes

Deep-Dish Apple Pie

Let the pie cool to eating temperature while you enjoy the main course. (Pictured on page 111.)

- 12 ounces (350g) frozen *or* fresh uncooked pastry
- 4 ounces (110g) caster sugar
- 2 tablespoons quick-cooking tapioca
- 1½ teaspoons ground cinnamon
- ¼ teaspoon finely grated lemon peel *or* dried lemon peel
- 2½ pounds (1kg125g) tinned sliced apples
- 2 tablespoons butter *or* margarine
- Sugar
- Single cream *or* vanilla ice cream (optional)

Thaw pastry if necessary. Roll out ⅛-inch (3mm) thick. Cut slits in the centre of the pastry.

Meanwhile, in a small mixing bowl stir together 4 ounces (110g) sugar, tapioca, cinnamon, and lemon peel. Drain *half* of apples. In a large mixing bowl combine drained and *undrained* apple slices and sugar mixture; toss together well to coat apples. Let stand 10 to 15 minutes.

Turn apple mixture into a medium casserole. Dot with butter or margarine. Place pastry over dish. Trim pastry to 1 inch (2.5cm) beyond the edge of the casserole dish. Fold under the extra pastry. Flute pastry to sides of dish, but not over edge. Sprinkle sugar lightly over pastry.

Bake in a 375°F (190°C) gas mark 5 oven for 55 to 60 minutes or until pastry is golden. Serve warm with cream or ice cream, if desired. Makes 6 servings.

Assembling time: 30 minutes
Cooking time: 55 to 60 minutes

Peach Crisp

1 ounce (25g) quick-cooking rolled oats
3 ounces (75g) packed soft brown sugar
1½ ounces (40g) plain flour
½ teaspoon ground cinnamon
2 ounces (50g) butter *or* margarine
1 pound (450g) peach slices
2 tablespoons caster sugar
2 ounces (50g) chopped walnuts
Vanilla ice cream (optional)

For topping, in a mixing bowl stir together oats, brown sugar, flour, and cinnamon. Cut in butter or margarine until mixture resembles coarse crumbs; set aside. Place peaches in an 8x8x2-inch (20x20x5cm) baking dish *or* an 8x1½-inch (20x4cm) round baking dish. Sprinkle sugar and oat mixture over peaches. Sprinkle nuts on top. Bake in a 350°F (180°C) gas mark 4 oven for 1 hour. Serve warm with ice cream, if desired. Makes 4 servings.

Assembling time: 15 minutes
Cooking time: 1 hour

Swiss Steak Dinner Timetable

About 2 hours before serving, prepare Oven Swiss Steak. Then, 1¼ hours before serving, place steak and 4 medium baking potatoes in the oven. Prepare Peach Crisp and add to oven.

Just before serving, cook green beans and top lettuce wedges with salad dressing. Remove dessert from oven; let cool during dinner. Remove meat and potatoes from the oven; transfer to a serving plate. Prepare sauce for meat.

Oven Swiss Steak

The rump steak bakes in a wonderfully seasoned, stewed tomato mixture.

1 pound (450g) top rump steak, cut ¾ inch (2cm) thick
2 tablespoons plain flour
¼ teaspoon celery salt
Dash pepper
2 tablespoons cooking oil
1 small onion
8 ounces (220g) tinned chopped tomatoes
2 teaspoons Worcestershire sauce
⅛ teaspoon garlic powder
1 tablespoon cold water
2 teaspoons cornflour

Cut beef into 4 serving-size pieces. Stir together flour, celery salt, and pepper. Use a meat mallet to pound the seasoned flour mixture into beef. In a 10-inch (25.5cm) frying pan cook meat on both sides in hot oil until brown.

Meanwhile, slice onion and separate into rings. In a bowl stir together onion, *undrained* tomatoes, Worcestershire sauce, and garlic powder. Transfer meat to a 10x6x2-inch (25.5x15x5cm) baking dish. Pour tomato mixture over meat. Cover dish with foil. Place in a 350°F (180°C) gas mark 4 oven (see photo 4, page 113). Bake for 1¼ hours or until tender.

Transfer meat to a serving plate (see photo 5, page 113). Skim fat from tomato mixture. For sauce, in a small saucepan stir together water and cornflour; stir in tomato mixture. Cook and stir until thickened and bubbly, then cook and stir 2 minutes more. Spoon sauce over meat. Makes 4 servings.

Assembling time: 20 minutes
Cooking time: 1¼ hours
Final preparation time: 5 minutes

▶ *Pictured opposite: Oven Swiss Steak, Peach Crisp*

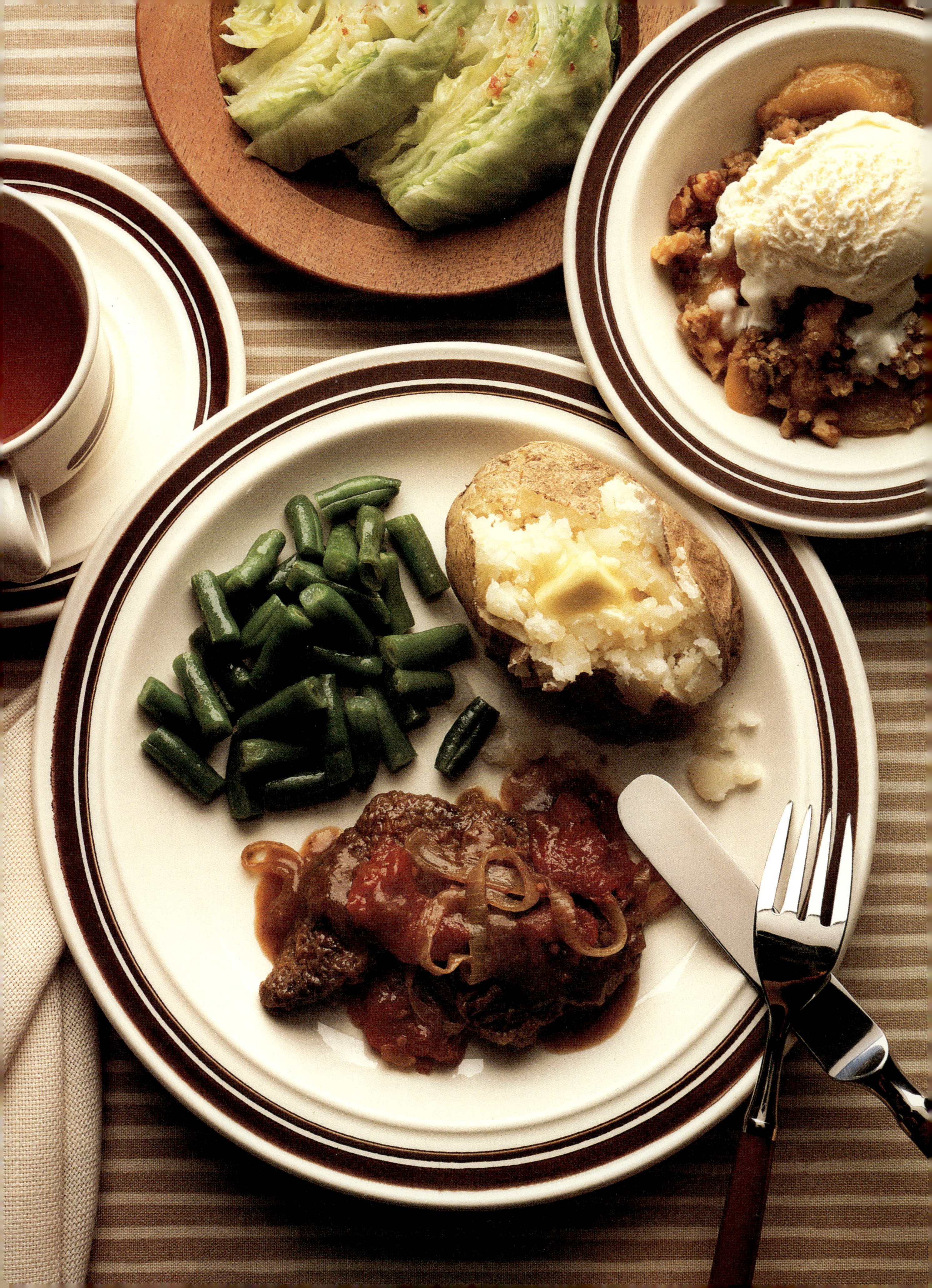

Special Helps

Shortcut Buying

Become a clever food shopper, and you can make every minute count. Supermarkets offer remarkable one-stop shopping. They're stocked with a wide variety of foods and they provide timesaving bakeries, delicatessens, and many non-food departments.

If you're interested in making the most of your shopping time, read on. These suggestions are meant to help you polish your food shopping skills.

Become a Planner
There's no way around it. A key to saving time at the supermarket is to plan ahead.

Prepare an organised shopping list—it'll save you considerable time by eliminating a lot of unnecessary backtracking at the supermarket. Group items on your list by food categories, such as dairy products, produce, tinned fruits and vegetables, cereals, meat, frozen foods, non-food items, staples, and baked goods.

Think about the layout of the supermarket where you shop. Then, organise your list following the layout. If the greengrocery counter is the first place on your route through the store, start your list with fresh fruits and vegetables.

Make out your shopping list at the same time as you plan your menus. By doing this, you will have the ingredients on hand for specific recipes you plan to prepare.

A shopping list also saves you time because it lists *all* the items you need. There's no chance of forgetting a needed ingredient and having to make a time-consuming return trip to the shop.

Jot It Down
Keep your shopping list handy to write down commonly used items as they run low. You'll never be disappointed because you ran out of an essential ingredient you "always have on hand" and "can't cook without" if you keep an up-to-date list of food needs.

Keep the list in a handy spot in your kitchen—that way, you'll always know where your shopping list can be found.

Also, remind family members to add to the list when they come across an item that needs replenishing on the next shopping trip.

Buy Convenience
Invest in convenience foods—those items that are partially or completely prepared.

When available, buy ingredients in the form you'll need for a recipe. For example, purchase ready-chopped vegetables, cut-up meat, chopped nuts, and breadcrumbs, if available. These convenient ingredients may cost you a little more—but remember, time is money!

There are other convenience foods that will save you time and work. Frozen juice concentrates; tinned soups; tinned meat, fish, and poultry; and quick-cooking rice are all timesaving ingredients you might include in your meals.

Shopping Time
To shop quickly, by-pass supermarket aisles that offer items you don't need.

A final timesaving reminder—shop when others don't! By avoiding the busy times of the week, such as weekends and after work, you won't have to queue for so long and you'll avoid crowded aisles.

Special Helps

The Know-How Of Freezing

Save both time and money simultaneously. How? Keep a stock of food in the freezer and eliminate time-consuming trips to the supermarket. And take advantage of a bargain. Buy food when it's on special offer, then store it in your freezer.

The secret to good freezer use is knowing the right way to wrap and store foods. After all, you've got an investment at stake, so keep food at its best.

Wrap It, Seal It, And Label It

To protect your frozen food, use moisture- and vapour-proof wrappings. These protective wrappings include the familiar silver foil, freezer wrap (heavy freezer paper), and polythene freezer bags.

Once the food is wrapped, seal packages with freezer tape. Buy the tape along with other freezing materials at your supermarket.

If you've ever gone to the freezer and pulled out an unlabelled mystery packet, you know the reason for labelling. The date is important, too. Foods have a storage time limit; for best flavour and quality, they should be used before the time has expired.

Keep an Up-to-date List

Another freezing must—keep an inventory of items in the freezer. A large sheet of paper and pencil attached to the freezer door will make the job easier. If you categorise the foods (beef, pork, bread, cake, etc.), you'll be able to quickly spot what you're looking for on the list. Remember to update the list with new purchases and cross off items as you use them.

Protect Your Meat Investment

Because meat is an expensive item, you need to take special care when freezing it. For short-time freezer storage (up to 2 weeks), it's alright to freeze fresh meat as it comes wrapped by the supermarket. Do check to make sure the wrapping hasn't been punctured. If it's been damaged, rewrap or overwrap with the freezing materials mentioned previously. Check out the easy wrapping directions at right. If you're not sure how soon you'll use the prepackaged meat, it's best to overwrap the store-wrapped packet.

Maintain the freezer temperature at 0° F. (-18°C) or lower. A thermometer placed in the freezer is a good way to check the temperature.

Wrap for Freezing The Easy Way

To wrap meat (and any other solid foods), use the simple technique shown above.

1. Place food in the centre of moisture- and vapourproof wrapping that's about 1½ times the circumference of the food. Bring the opposite sides of wrapping together.

2. Fold edges down in a series of locked folds. Press wrapping tightly against meat, pressing out air.

3. Crease the ends into points.

4. Fold the ends up snugly to the centre of the packet; seal with freezer tape. Label.

How Long Can You Store Meat?

Freeze fresh, uncooked meat and poultry at 0° F (-18°C). Store:
- beef steaks and joints 6 to 12 months;
- pork chops 3 to 4 months;
- pork and veal joints 4 to 8 months;
- lamb chops and joints 6 to 9 months;
- minced meats 3 to 4 months;
- chicken pieces 9 months;
- turkey pieces 6 months;
- giblets 3 to 4 months;
- whole chickens and turkeys 12 months.

Nutrition Analysis Chart

Use these analyses to compare nutritional values of different recipes. This information was calculated using Agriculture Handbook Number 456, published by the United States Department of Agriculture, as the primary source. Figures are based on the ingredients used in the American version of each recipe.

In compiling the nutrition analyses, we made the following assumptions:
- For all of the main-dish meat recipes, the nutrition analyses were calculated using weights or measures for cooked meat.
- Garnishes and optional ingredients were not included in the nutrition analyses.
- If a marinade was brushed over a food during cooking, the analysis includes all of the marinade.
- When two ingredient options appear in a recipe, calculations were made using the first one.
- For ingredients of variable weight (such as "2½- to 3-pound (1kg125g to 1kg350g) chicken") or for recipes with a serving range ("Makes 4 to 6 servings"), calculations were made using the first figure.

	Calories	Protein (g)	Carbohydrate (g)	Fat (g)	Sodium (mg)	Potassium (mg)	Protein	Vitamin A	Vitamin C	Thiamine	Riboflavin	Niacin	Calcium	Iron
Eggs and Cheese														
Beer-Cheese Soup (p. 44)	320	16	21	17	707	106	25	14	1	14	20	9	40	7
Broccoli Frittata (p. 60)	254	15	4	20	319	232	23	46	46	8	21	2	19	13
Courgette Lasagne (p. 106)	323	18	29	15	273	375	27	28	36	22	22	14	31	10
Easy Farmer's Breakfast (p. 63)	394	19	18	27	504	388	29	20	36	21	20	10	8	19
Ham and Potato Quiche (p. 95)	370	17	20	25	655	242	27	22	4	12	23	7	29	12
Hearty Italian Quiche (p. 92)	354	14	18	25	491	190	22	12	3	15	20	9	19	9
Pepperoni Frittata (p. 63)	457	20	11	37	1312	233	30	30	0	12	26	10	10	16
Quiche in Pasta Crust (p. 94)	384	21	26	21	455	223	33	18	1	23	27	12	40	13
Spaghetti Sauce Lasagne (p. 108)	359	22	33	15	847	137	34	14	2	19	24	9	30	11
Three-Cheese Quiche (p. 94)	387	16	21	27	481	183	25	14	1	12	24	5	29	8
Turkey Quiche (p. 95)	352	25	25	17	674	302	39	17	0	10	26	16	39	14
Fish and Seafood														
California Fish Salad (p. 69)	313	22	11	21	379	717	34	15	26	9	11	12	21	10
Crunchy Tuna Salad (p. 16)	276	20	12	17	523	422	30	12	40	8	14	37	7	12
Fish Chowder (p. 42)	397	26	18	24	230	728	40	90	48	13	28	14	27	7
Fish with Cream Sauce (p. 68)	217	27	4	9	234	434	41	10	11	6	8	14	5	6
Italian-Style Fish (p. 68)	153	20	5	6	489	436	30	14	8	7	7	13	14	7
No-Chop Prawn Stir-Fry (p. 101)	366	24	38	13	1463	673	37	18	44	15	18	37	12	21
Orange-Poached Fish (p. 66)	312	21	53	1	246	858	33	162	63	25	8	21	12	16
Oven-Fried Fish (p. 51)	283	29	9	13	372	423	45	11	0	9	11	17	5	9
Prawn Frittata (p. 62)	246	20	5	17	367	289	30	38	60	8	21	5	14	18
Prawns in Cheddar Sauce (p. 83)	439	21	28	26	542	248	32	20	15	20	20	14	28	16
Salmon Potato Salad (p. 17)	553	32	36	32	1763	1275	49	15	60	15	23	57	30	22
Salmon Stroganoff Frying Pan Supper (p. 36)	343	23	24	17	880	502	35	21	14	20	20	44	26	12
Scallops and Mange Tout (p. 98)	340	25	40	8	897	618	38	11	26	24	8	16	13	26

	Calories	Protein (g)	Carbohydrate (g)	Fat (g)	Sodium (mg)	Potassium (mg)	Protein	Vitamin A	Vitamin C	Thiamine	Riboflavin	Niacin	Calcium	Iron
Fish and Seafood *(continued)*														
Seafood and Wild Rice Salad (p. 23)	330	21	33	13	1063	275	32	7	22	12	6	15	13	21
Seafood Louis (p. 14)	478	18	24	37	564	752	28	41	72	13	17	12	12	23
Tuna-Broccoli-Sauced Pastry (p. 22)	320	20	20	18	1018	352	31	23	45	12	15	38	9	11
Tuna-Spaghetti Frying Pan Supper (p. 38)	449	25	34	24	1149	522	38	40	86	23	24	48	11	14
Wine-Sauced Fish Steaks (p. 69)	511	33	30	27	807	722	50	24	10	38	8	68	2	14
Meats														
Barbecue-Style Pork Roast (p. 54)	312	29	10	16	311	625	45	19	138	45	20	30	4	24
Barley-Sausage Frying Pan Supper (p. 39)	469	21	28	31	1953	412	33	44	18	24	16	18	15	18
Scone-Topped Frying Pan Supper (p. 75)	446	20	42	22	1359	477	31	23	12	16	26	24	15	24
Bratwurst-Potato Chowder (p. 44)	436	19	37	24	1256	862	30	56	32	20	33	18	28	14
Cheese and Pastrami Hoagies (p. 10)	420	19	33	23	849	176	30	13	7	15	19	12	23	15
Chilli-Bean Dish (p. 75)	368	25	21	21	842	587	38	51	42	12	20	22	25	21
Corned Beef and Brussels Sprouts (p. 57)	483	27	24	31	968	698	42	6	106	12	17	17	4	23
Cranberry-Peach Ham (p. 83)	519	21	65	19	1262	482	32	92	24	38	13	25	4	21
Creamed Peas and Beef (p. 77)	556	21	36	36	1061	400	33	22	16	41	25	24	9	22
Dilled Meat and Potato Chowder (p. 76)	261	17	18	13	449	446	26	16	17	11	17	19	10	13
Easy Corned Beef Stroganoff (p. 25)	494	33	36	24	1235	303	50	16	13	31	32	35	11	33
Easy Reubens (p. 11)	512	23	32	33	1598	241	36	7	15	12	18	12	23	18
Family-Size Hero Sandwich (p. 8)	489	20	50	23	1241	465	31	14	43	24	13	16	8	17
Frying Pan Stuffed Peppers (p. 74)	352	23	21	20	668	547	35	45	114	15	19	21	23	19
German-Style Pot Roast (p. 57)	646	31	22	48	327	722	48	108	31	11	17	30	4	26
Ham and Apricot Kababs (p. 88)	521	25	50	25	983	474	38	4	87	41	15	22	3	23
Ham and Macaroni Coleslaw (p. 17)	757	24	49	53	791	467	37	12	44	43	28	22	31	18
Ham and Pecan Stir-Fry (p. 102)	518	19	38	32	1413	427	29	4	95	42	13	19	4	21
Ham and Prawn Creole (p. 20)	367	25	43	10	552	801	38	50	93	34	12	29	8	31
Ham and Spaetzle Frying Pan Supper (p. 39)	473	23	39	25	1414	465	36	15	16	42	26	25	11	23
Hearty Open Sandwiches (p. 73)	405	21	38	20	1137	440	32	23	11	13	19	19	13	19
Herbed Breaded Pork Chops (p. 50)	332	25	17	18	619	301	38	0	4	57	19	29	5	19
Individual Ham Loaves (p. 31)	467	31	14	31	1173	417	47	13	14	61	22	26	6	26
Macaroni-Beef Supper (p. 37)	587	30	39	35	1438	459	45	14	9	22	25	34	10	28
Meat and Potato Kababs (p. 88)	682	24	26	54	1904	739	36	1	51	12	16	27	5	25
Meaty Cream Cheese Stroganoff (p. 74)	454	22	26	29	301	314	33	32	5	14	25	22	9	17
Mexicali Fry Up (p. 34)	347	15	36	16	549	485	23	25	45	15	13	13	18	18
Mexican Cannelloni (p. 109)	647	29	50	37	2304	721	45	19	12	29	27	31	21	29
Minced Meat Freezer Base (p.72)	170	13	4	11	177	199	21	15	3	5	8	14	2	11
Mustard-Sauced Liver (p. 103)	357	24	20	20	844	376	36	811	42	16	189	65	2	40
Old-Fashioned Meat Loaf (p. 30)	336	24	14	20	541	398	38	10	7	11	17	24	7	20
Oriental Beef (p. 76)	420	25	33	20	1498	461	38	27	25	21	18	27	6	26
Oven Swiss Steak (p. 116)	302	23	10	19	253	415	36	11	21	8	13	25	2	18
Penne with Italian Sauce (p. 82)	466	23	44	22	740	707	35	41	54	48	25	37	8	26
Pizza Cannelloni (p. 109)	494	28	42	23	952	275	43	7	5	23	20	27	22	22

Nutrition Analysis Chart

	Per Serving						U.S. Recommended Daily Allowances Per Serving (%)							
	Calories	Protein (g)	Carbohydrate (g)	Fat (g)	Sodium (mg)	Potassium (mg)	Protein	Vitamin A	Vitamin C	Thiamine	Riboflavin	Niacin	Calcium	Iron
Meats (continued)														
Pizza-Style Meat Loaf (p. 28)	368	27	15	22	567	276	41	5	2	8	16	24	13	21
Saucy Orange Beef (p. 82)	372	21	40	13	1145	481	32	9	63	16	14	25	5	22
Sausage-Onion Stir-Fry (p. 103)	568	25	38	33	2553	627	38	1	77	32	19	29	6	27
Sausage-Vegetable Stew (p. 25)	509	19	36	32	1877	693	29	165	40	26	21	27	4	23
Savoury Beef-Vegetable Soup (p. 45)	293	19	16	17	858	498	28	73	21	11	15	23	6	15
Spicy Pork Kababs (p. 89)	392	19	22	26	1035	486	29	4	29	32	16	20	5	20
Spinach and Lamb Loaf (p. 31)	374	25	10	26	374	444	38	80	23	14	25	22	17	15
Stew with Potato Topper (p. 80)	459	24	34	26	734	803	36	186	24	10	18	22	10	24
Stuffed Pitta Pockets (p. 10)	309	16	15	20	397	304	25	13	16	7	12	10	23	10
Sweet-Sour Beef and Vegetable Salad (p. 77)	285	17	24	15	245	775	27	156	93	13	24	22	12	29
Teriyaki-Sauced Beef and Courgette (p. 102)	340	21	27	16	1171	457	32	7	39	14	15	26	5	21
Veal Parmigiano (p. 51)	411	29	18	24	867	255	45	14	0	7	21	20	28	18
Zesty Pork Loaves (p. 30)	457	28	10	33	628	273	43	10	0	32	24	20	26	18
Poultry														
Chicken and Bulgur Frying Pan Supper (p. 36)	336	25	39	10	485	494	39	43	87	14	15	40	7	16
Chicken and Corkscrew Macaroni (p. 23)	449	32	46	15	1368	362	50	39	52	35	29	42	24	19
Chicken and Fruit Salad (p. 16)	493	22	38	30	430	850	34	32	86	12	20	26	8	18
Chicken Lasagne (p. 108)	349	21	28	17	617	290	32	18	17	20	24	21	17	10
Chicken Liver Stir-Fry (p. 101)	381	29	35	12	286	338	44	215	115	33	145	63	4	49
Chicken-Mushroom Frittata (p. 62)	232	21	3	14	260	273	33	19	5	8	22	18	7	14
Cranberry-Orange Turkey Stir-Fry (p. 100)	342	34	37	8	1065	761	53	11	38	15	21	54	8	20
Deli Salad Sandwiches (p. 10)	465	16	37	29	537	327	25	5	11	22	13	18	7	14
Easy Chicken Stir-Fry (p. 100)	231	20	15	10	1044	248	31	30	91	8	18	36	5	12
Freezer-to-Table Frying Pan Supper (p. 37)	386	31	41	11	1500	649	47	172	19	29	27	43	8	29
Herbed Broccoli Soup (p. 45)	297	29	19	12	574	595	45	45	88	12	29	33	33	10
Italian Chicken Kababs (p. 89)	403	32	8	27	839	408	49	4	50	12	37	75	3	14
Italian-Seasoned Chicken Thighs (p. 50)	388	31	15	22	376	362	48	10	0	9	33	39	2	18
Lemon-Herbed Chicken (p. 112)	227	29	1	11	124	12	44	26	6	7	34	43	2	16
Oven-Fried Chicken (p. 48)	271	28	17	9	252	67	42	35	9	20	45	46	4	18
Potato Shell Turkey Pie (p. 22)	419	19	28	26	698	679	29	59	16	8	16	21	18	11
Rush Hour Simmer Dinner (p. 38)	413	30	37	16	847	354	46	137	22	33	19	42	5	19
Sweet 'n' Sour Chicken Dinner (p. 56)	381	31	56	4	534	473	48	164	79	20	18	61	8	22
Teriyaki Chicken Kababs (p. 86)	335	31	11	17	1347	331	48	30	77	8	18	58	6	16
Turkey Club Sandwiches (p. 11)	505	35	67	12	746	736	53	8	11	22	24	41	31	20
Turkey Roast with Sweet Potatoes (p. 56)	459	32	39	19	109	698	49	153	31	12	19	33	5	19
Miscellaneous														
Baked Squash with Peas (p. 115)	114	5	27		246	772	7	50	57	13	14	9	6	11
Deep-Dish Apple Pie (p. 115)	345	2	55	14	234	135	3	4	3	9	5	5	1	7
Peach Crisp (p. 116)	424	4	64	19	148	294	7	24	76	10	6	7	4	12

Index

A-B

Apple Pie, Deep-Dish, 115
Apricot Kababs, Ham and, 88
Baked Squash with Peas, 115
Barbecue-Style Pork Roast, 54
Barley-Sausage Frying Pan
    Supper, 39
Beef
    Cheese and Pastrami
        Hoagies, 10
    German-Style Pot Roast, 57
    Meat and Potato Kababs, 88
    Oven Swiss Steak, 116
    Saucy Orange Beef, 82
    Stew with Potato Topper, 80
    Stuffed Pitta Pockets, 10
    Teriyaki-Sauced Beef and
        Courgette, 102
Beef, Corned
    Corned Beef and Brussels
        Sprouts, 57
    Easy Corned Beef
        Stroganoff, 25
    Easy Reubens, 11
Beef, Minced
    Chilli-Bean Dish, 75
    Creamed Peas and Beef, 77
    Dilled Meat and Potato
        Chowder, 76
    Frying Pan Stuffed
        Peppers, 74
    Hearty Open Sandwiches, 73
    Macaroni-Beef Supper, 37
    Meaty Cream Cheese
        Stroganoff, 74
    Minced Meat Freezer Base, 72
    Old-Fashioned Meat Loaf, 30
    Oriental Beef, 76
    Penne with Italian Sauce, 82
    Pizza Cannelloni, 109
    Pizza-Style Meat Loaf, 28
    Savoury Beef-Vegetable
        Soup, 45
    Scone-Topped Frying Pan
        Supper, 75
    Sweet-Sour Beef and
        Vegetable Salad, 77

Beer-Cheese Soup, 44
Bratwurst-Potato Chowder, 44
Breaking up tinned meat, 21
Broccoli
    Broccoli Frittata, 60
    Tuna-Broccoli-Sauced
        Pastry, 22
Brussels Sprouts, Corned Beef
    and, 57
Bulgur Frying Pan Supper,
    Chicken and, 36

C

California Fish Salad, 69
Cannelloni
    Mexican Cannelloni, 109
    Pizza Cannelloni, 109
Casseroles
    Chicken Lasagne, 108
    Courgette Lasagne, 106
    Mexican Cannelloni, 109
    Pizza Cannelloni, 109
    Spaghetti Sauce Lasagne, 108
Cheese
    Beer-Cheese Soup, 44
    Cheese and Pastrami
        Hoagies, 10
    Chicken Lasagne, 108
    Courgette Lasagne, 106
    Spaghetti Sauce Lasagne, 108
    Three-Cheese Quiche, 94
Chicken
    Chicken and Bulgur Frying
        Pan Supper, 36
    Chicken and Corkscrew
        Macaroni, 23
    Chicken and Fruit Salad, 16
    Chicken Lasagne, 108
    Chicken-Mushroom Frittata, 62
    Coating chicken pieces, 49
    Cranberry-Orange Turkey
        Stir-Fry, 100
    Cutting chicken strips, 86

Chicken *(continued)*
    Cutting up chicken, 49
    Deli Salad Sandwiches, 10
    Easy Chicken Stir-Fry, 100
    Freezer-to-Table Frying Pan
        Supper, 37
    Herbed Broccoli Soup, 45
    Italian Chicken Kababs, 89
    Italian-Seasoned Chicken
        Thighs, 50
    Lemon-Herbed Chicken, 112
    Oven-Fried Chicken, 48
    Rush Hour Simmer Dinner, 38
    Sweet 'n' Sour Chicken
        Dinner, 56
    Teriyaki Chicken Kababs, 86
    Turkey Quiche, 95
Chicken Liver Stir-Fry, 101
Chilli-Bean Dish, 75
Chowder, Dilled Meat and
    Potato, 76
Corned Beef and Brussels
    Sprouts, 57
Courgette
    Courgette Lasagne, 106
    Teriyaki-Sauced Beef and
        Courgette, 102
Crab
    Seafood and Wild Rice
        Salad, 23
    Seafood Louis, 14
Cranberry-Orange Turkey
    Stir-Fry, 100
Cranberry-Peach Ham, 83
Creamed Peas and Beef, 77
Creole, Ham and Prawn, 20
Crunchy Tuna Salad, 16
Crushing cereal, 48
Cutting up meat, 21

D-G

Deep-Dish Apple Pie, 115
Deli Salad Sandwiches, 10
Desserts
    Deep-Dish Apple Pie, 115
    Peach Crisp, 116

Index

Dilled Meat and Potato Chowder, 76
Draining tinned foods, 21
Easy Chicken Stir-Fry, 100
Easy Corned Beef Stroganoff, 25
Easy Farmer's Breakfast, 63
Easy Reubens, 11
Eggs
   Beating eggs lightly, 60
   Broccoli Frittata, 60
   Chicken-Mushroom Frittata, 62
   Easy Farmer's Breakfast, 63
   Pepperoni Frittata, 63
   Prawn Frittata, 62
   Quick-cooling hard-cooked eggs, 14
Family-Size Hero Sandwich, 8
Fish
   Breaking up tinned fish, 21
   California Fish Salad, 69
   Fish Chowder, 42
   Fish with Cream Sauce, 68
   Italian-Style Fish, 68
   Orange-Poached Fish, 66
   Oven-Fried Fish, 51
   Seafood Louis, 14
   Testing fish for degree of cooking, 67
   Wine-Sauced Fish Steaks, 69
Freezer Base, Minced Meat, 72
Freezer-to-Table Frying Pan Supper, 37
Freezing meat, 120–121
Frittatas
   Broccoli Frittata, 60
   Chicken-Mushroom Frittata, 62
   Easy Farmer's Breakfast, 63
   Pepperoni Frittata, 63
   Prawn Frittata, 62
Frying Pan Dishes
   Barley-Sausage Frying Pan Supper, 39
   Chicken and Bulgur Frying Pan Supper, 36
   Freezer-to-Table Frying Pan Supper, 37

Frying Pan Dishes *(continued)*
   Frying Pan Stuffed Peppers, 74
   Ham and Spaetzle Frying Pan Supper, 39
   Macaroni-Beef Supper, 37
   Mexicali Fry Up, 34
   Rush Hour Simmer Dinner, 38
   Salmon Stroganoff Frying Pan Supper, 36
   Tuna-Spaghetti Frying Pan Supper, 38
Frying Pan Stuffed Peppers, 74
German-Style Pot Roast, 57

H-K

Ham
   Cranberry-Peach Ham, 83
   Deli Salad Sandwiches, 10
   Easy Farmer's Breakfast, 63
   Family-Size Hero Sandwich, 8
   Ham and Apricot Kababs, 88
   Ham and Macaroni Coleslaw, 17
   Ham and Pecan Stir-Fry, 102
   Ham and Potato Quiche, 95
   Ham and Prawn Creole, 20
   Ham and Spaetzle Frying Pan Supper, 39
   Herbed Broccoli Soup, 45
   Individual Ham Loaves, 31
   Stuffed Pitta Pockets, 10
Hearty Italian Quiche, 92
Hearty Open Sandwiches, 73
Herbed Breaded Pork Chops, 50
Herbed Broccoli Soup, 45
Herbed Chicken, Lemon-, 112
Individual Ham Loaves, 31
Italian Chicken Kababs, 89
Italian-Seasoned Chicken Thighs, 50
Italian-Style Fish, 68

Kababs
   Ham and Apricot Kababs, 88
   Italian Chicken Kababs, 89
   Meat and Potato Kababs, 88
   Spicy Pork Kababs, 89
   Teriyaki Chicken Kababs, 86
   Threading kababs, 87

L-O

Lamb
   Meat and Potato Kababs, 88
   Spinach and Lamb Loaf, 31
Lasagne
   Chicken Lasagne, 108
   Courgette Lasagne, 106
   Spaghetti Sauce Lasagne, 108
Lemon-Herbed Chicken, 112
Liver, Mustard-Sauced, 103
Macaroni-Beef Supper, 37
Macaroni Coleslaw, Ham and, 17
Making a cucumber twist garnish, 67
Making breadcrumbs, 72
Mange Toute, Scallops and, 98
Measuring grilling distance, 87
Meat and Potato Kababs, 88
Meat Loaves
   Individual Ham Loaves, 31
   Old-Fashioned Meat Loaf, 30
   Pizza-Style Meat Loaf, 28
   Shaping meat loaves, 28–29
   Spinach and Lamb Loaf, 31
   Zesty Pork Loaves, 30
Meaty Cream Cheese Stroganoff, 74
Mexicali Fry Up, 34
Mexican Cannelloni, 109
Minced Meat Freezer Base, 72
Mushroom Frittata, Chicken-, 62
Mustard-Sauced Liver, 103
No-Chop Prawn Stir-Fry, 101
Old-Fashioned Meat Loaf, 30
Oranges
   Cranberry-Orange Turkey Stir-Fry, 100

Oranges *(continued)*
   Making an orange twist garnish, 67
   Orange-Poached Fish, 66
   Saucy Orange Beef, 82
Oriental Beef, 76
Oven-Fried Chicken, 48
Oven-Fried Fish, 51
Oven Swiss Steak, 116

P-R

Parmigiano, Veal, 51
Pasta
   Chicken and Corkscrew Macaroni, 23
   Chicken Lasagne, 108
   Courgette Lasagne, 106
   Ham and Macaroni Coleslaw, 17
   Ham and Spaetzle Frying Pan Supper, 39
   Mexican Cannelloni, 109
   Penne with Italian Sauce, 82
   Pizza Cannelloni, 109
   Quiche in Pasta Crust, 94
   Rush Hour Simmer Dinner, 38
   Spaghetti Sauce Lasagne, 108
   Testing for degree of cooking, 107
   Tuna-Spaghetti Frying Pan Supper, 38
Pastrami Hoagies, Cheese and, 10
Peaches
   Cranberry-Peach Ham, 83
   Peach Crisp, 116
Peas
   Baked Squash with Peas, 115
   Creamed Peas and Beef, 77
Penne with Italian Sauce, 82
Pepperoni Frittata, 63
Pies, Dessert
   Deep-Dish Apple Pie, 115

Pies, Main-Dish
   Ham and Potato Quiche, 95
   Hearty Italian Quiche, 92
   Potato Shell Turkey Pie, 22
   Quiche in Pasta Crust, 94
   Three-Cheese Quiche, 94
   Turkey Quiche, 95
Pizza Cannelloni, 109
Pizza-Style Meat Loaf, 28
Poached Fish, Orange-, 66
Pork
   Barbecue-Style Pork Roast, 54
   Herbed Breaded Pork Chops, 50
   Spicy Pork Kababs, 89
   Stew with Potato Topper, 80
Pork, Minced
   Minced Meat Freezer Base, 72
   Zesty Pork Loaves, 30
Potatoes
   Bratwurst-Potato Chowder, 44
   Dilled Meat and Potato Chowder, 76
   Easy Farmer's Breakfast, 63
   Ham and Potato Quiche, 95
   Meat and Potato Kababs, 88
   Potato Shell Turkey Pie, 22
   Salmon Potato Salad, 17
   Stew with Potato Topper, 80
   Turkey Roast with Sweet Potatoes, 56
Prawns
   Ham and Prawn Creole, 20
   No-Chop Prawn Stir-Fry, 101
   Prawn Frittata, 62
   Prawns in Cheddar Sauce, 83
   Seafood and Wild Rice Salad, 23
   Seafood Louis, 14
   Thawing frozen prawns, 20
Preparing a papaya, 86

Quiches
   Ham and Potato Quiche, 95
   Hearty Italian Quiche, 92
   Preparing pastry case, 92
   Quiche in Pasta Crust, 94
   Testing for degree of cooking, 93
   Three-Cheese Quiche, 94
   Turkey Quiche, 95
Quick-cooling foods, 81
Reubens, Easy, 11
Rush Hour Simmer Dinner, 38

S

Salads
   California Fish Salad, 69
   Chicken and Fruit Salad, 16
   Crunchy Tuna Salad, 16
   Ham and Macaroni Coleslaw, 17
   Salmon Potato Salad, 17
   Seafood and Wild Rice Salad, 23
   Seafood Louis, 14
   Sweet-Sour Beef and Vegetable Salad, 77
Salmon
   Salmon Potato Salad, 17
   Salmon Stroganoff Frying Pan Supper, 36
Sandwiches
   Cheese and Pastrami Hoagies, 10
   Deli Salad Sandwiches, 10
   Easy Reubens, 11
   Family-Size Hero Sandwich, 8
   Hearty Open Sandwiches, 73
   Stuffed Pitta Pockets, 10
   Turkey Club Sandwiches, 11
Saucy Orange Beef, 82
Sausage
   Barley-Sausage Frying Pan Supper, 39
   Bratwurst-Potato Chowder, 44

Index

Sausage *(continued)*
  Family-Size Hero Sandwich, 8
  Hearty Italian Quiche, 92
  Mexicali Fry Up, 34
  Mexican Cannelloni, 109
  Penne with Italian Sauce, 82
  Pepperoni Frittata, 63
  Sausage-Onion Stir-Fry, 103
  Sausage-Vegetable Stew, 25
Savoury Beef-Vegetable Soup, 45
Scallops and Mange Tout, 98
Scone-Topped Frying Pan Supper, 75
Seafood
  Seafood and Wild Rice Salad, 23
  Seafood Louis, 14
Skimming fat from cooking liquid, 55
Slow Cooker Recipes
  Assembling slow cooker dishes, 55
  Barbecue-Style Pork Roast, 54
  Corned Beef and Brussels Sprouts, 57
  German-Style Pot Roast, 57
  Sweet 'n' Sour Chicken Dinner, 56
  Turkey Roast with Sweet Potatoes, 56
Soups
  Beer-Cheese Soup, 44
  Bratwurst-Potato Chowder, 44
  Fish Chowder, 42
  Herbed Broccoli Soup, 45
  Savoury Beef-Vegetable Soup, 45
Spaghetti Sauce Lasagne, 108
Spicy Pork Kababs, 89
Spinach and Lamb Loaf, 31
Spooning off excess fat, 29
Squash with Peas, Baked, 115
Stews
  Sausage-Vegetable Stew, 25
  Stew with Potato Topper, 80

Stir-Fry Recipes
  Adding oil to a hot wok or frying pan, 98
  Chicken Liver Stir-Fry, 101
  Cranberry-Orange Turkey Stir-Fry, 100
  Easy Chicken Stir-Fry, 100
  Ham and Pecan Stir-Fry, 102
  Mustard-Sauced Liver, 103
  No-Chop Prawn Stir-Fry, 101
  Sausage-Onion Stir-Fry, 103
  Scallops and Mange Tout, 98
  Stir-frying techniques, 99
  Teriyaki-Sauced Beef and Courgette, 102
Stroganoff
  Easy Corned Beef Stroganoff, 25
  Meaty Cream Cheese Stroganoff, 74
  Salmon Stroganoff Frying Pan Supper, 36
Stuffed Pitta Pockets, 10
Sweet 'n' Sour Chicken Dinner, 56
Sweet-Sour Beef and Vegetable Salad, 77
Swiss Steak, Oven, 116

T-Z

Teriyaki Chicken Kababs, 86
Teriyaki-Sauced Beef and Courgette, 102
Thickening with flour, 43
Three-Cheese Quiche, 94
Tuna
  Crunchy Tuna Salad, 16
  Tuna Broccoli Sauced Pastry, 22
  Tuna-Spaghetti Frying Pan Supper, 38
Turkey
  Chicken Lasagne, 108
  Cranberry-Orange Turkey Stir-Fry, 100

Turkey *(continued)*
  Herbed Broccoli Soup, 45
  Potato Shell Turkey Pie, 22
  Turkey Club Sandwiches, 11
  Turkey Quiche, 95
  Turkey Roast with Sweet Potatoes, 56
Using an oven cooking bag, 112–113
Veal Parmigiano, 51
Vegetables
  Baked Squash with Peas, 115
  Chopping an onion, 34
  Cutting up tinned tomatoes, 20
  Sausage-Vegetable Stew, 25
  Savoury Beef-Vegetable Soup, 45
  Shredding lettuce or cabbage, 14
  Slicing a tomato, 9
  Slicing vegetables, 66
  Thawing frozen vegetables, 20
Wild Rice Salad, Seafood and, 23
Wine-Sauced Fish Steaks, 69
Zesty Pork Loaves, 30

Tips

A Chilling Fact, 16
Buying Frozen Fish, 68
Cook Them Well Done, 30
Homemade Convenience, 50
Hot Breads, 17
Keep It Covered, 57
Meat Loaf Microwave Tips, 31
Microwave Directions, 28
Oven Meal Timetable, 114
Quick Fruit Salads, 22
Swiss Steak Dinner Timetable, 116
Thawing the Minced Meat Freezer Base, 75